Triumph and Tragedy in Central America

by Patrick O'Connor

A History of the Conservative Baptist Movement in Central America – 1950 to 2000

O'Connor, Patrick
White Unto Harvest:
Triumph and Tragedy in Central America
1st edition

ISBN: 0-9706859-9-8

Published by:

Enable! Media
16076 NW Joscelyn St.
Beaverton, OR 97006

www.servants-inc.org/enable-media

To contact publisher: enable-media@servants-inc.org

To contact author: patrick@servants-inc.org

Cover design by Rachel Aw

To all of the CB missionaries
who have served in Central America –
past, present and future

Prepared on Behalf of Mission to the
Americas' 50th Anniversary – 2000

"Do you not say,

'There are yet four months,

and then comes the harvest'?

Behold, I say to you, lift up your eyes,

and look to the fields,

that they are white for harvest."

John 4:35 (NAS)

Contents

Preface and Introduction

History is a bit like tilling the soil. Some events seem to need to settle into time and lie fallow for a season until some eager searcher uncovers them and recognizes pearls of wisdom buried in the dust. That may not happen for decades, even lifetimes. But it will never happen unless we first record history and sift through it.

For this reason I have written this history of the CB movement in Central America. In that history is oftentimes neither read nor appreciated until decades after it takes place, I have prepared this text for the next generation. Perhaps 20 years or so from now, new missionaries to Central America may come across this book and (hopefully) think, "Wow, this is just what I needed. Now I can learn something from what happened during the early years!" It is mostly for such a missionary and for such a

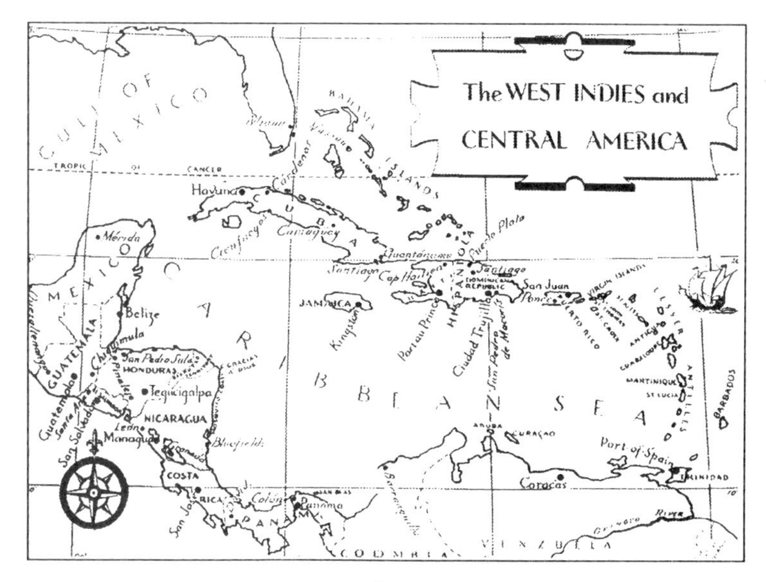

time that this text is prepared. But for those who pick it up in the meantime, I also hope that this text will stimulate thinking about the missionary models we choose and how we collectively minister cross-culturally.

Throughout the text, I took the liberty of using the pen (er...keyboard) to bring up "Food for Thought" – indicated by the "✒" symbols – to indicate important concepts and to suggest appropriate perspectives and applications reflecting on how, or how not, past missionary models may serve us today. While historical review naturally involves interpretation and commentary, or what historians call analysis and synthesis, I have tried to be objective. I have attempted to create interaction with the reader and to provoke thought with regard to our past and our future. Thus, this book is much more than a historical narrative – it serves us by encouraging us to consider adjustments for the future. It is written to affirm our past, yet to learn from it.

While I have attempted not to bring out too much "dirty laundry" from our collective past, I have dealt matter-of-factly with struggles experienced by our missionaries. I have written about the tragedies and not just the triumphs. It is not my intent to dwell on the negative, but to give a fair consideration to the record. I believe that we are strong enough organizationally as a mission to recognize both our victories and our disappointments. To cite only our successes would be historical revisionism.

This text is not meant to be an exhaustive study of the subject. Rather, it is an overview. It is an effort to immortalize, through the printed page, many of our own CB heroes of the faith who have served under our banner. The report covers the Caribbean and parts of southern and central Mexico as part of Central America, but not northern Mexico, due to the constraints of time, information and energy.

When writing about events prior to 1994, I used our former name, the Conservative Baptist Home Mission Society (CBHMS). When writing about events after the name change in 1994, I used the Mission's new name, Mission to the Americas (MTA).

Note that the opinions expressed are my own and do not necessarily reflect those of the Mission. Also, if you find any errors in this report relating to dates and historical details, feel free to pass the information on to the Mission, the Publisher, or to me. I apologize in advance for any inaccuracies that might have slipped in.

Finally, many thanks to Dick Falconer, Cory Keith, Mary Ann Jeffreys, Anne Thiessen and my mother, Dorothy O'Connor, who painstakingly proofed the document and gave me valuable suggestions toward its preparation. And also, many thanks to my Publisher, Dale Aufrecht with ***Enable! Media***, for seeing this project through to the end.

Patrick O'Connor
Copán Ruins, Honduras

October, 2001

Publisher's Note: About the Graphics – Many of the pictures used in this book were provided by the subjects or their families. Many thanks for the photographs. Historical photos also came from the archives of ***The Challenge***, published by the Conservative Baptist Home Mission Society. Maps illustrating individual countries courtesy of The General Libraries, The University of Texas at Austin.

Southern Mexico

Manis and Jane Ruegsegger

Nestled in a southern Mexican state above a hill overlooking Cuixtla, Oaxaca, lay two graves – those of Manis and Jane Ruegsegger. If you talk with locals or with folks from many of the isolated, hard-to-get-to mountain communities scattered throughout this southern Mexican area, they would tell you long and colorful stories of two saints and their travels for more than 36 years as CBHMS missionaries.

The locals would tell you of their all-night serenade to Jane upon her passing or of how many of them were brought into this world by the hands of Manis. They would tell you of how these two godly Bible translators-turned-medical doctors entered into their community in the winter of 1951. They would speak of how Manis and Jane with their two children – son Ron and daughter Gerry – arrived full of youthful energy and how, after more than three decades (32 years for Jane and 36 years for Manis), they endured with equal energy. The locals would tell you how the Ruegseggers lived with the people in dirt-floored, mud homes

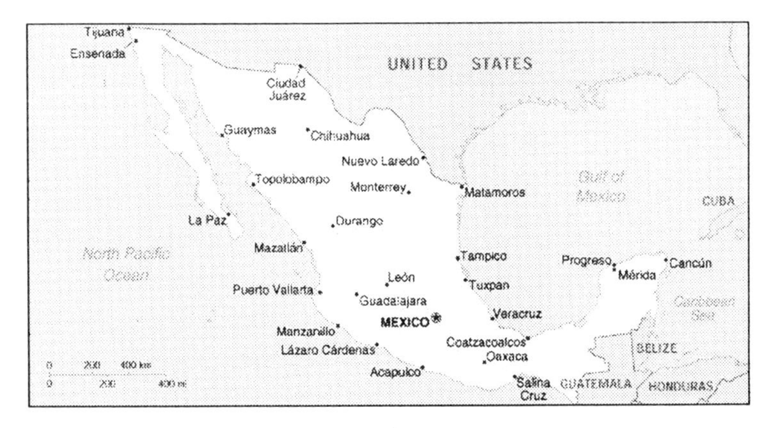

and how they lived simply, presenting the love of Christ with humility.

Manis and Jane Ruegsegger.

Manis and Jane Ruegsegger were appointed as one of the early CBHMS missionaries in the fall of 1950 – merely months after the founding of the society. CBHMS board member Claude Moffitt, who was a real recruiter for the Mission during those days, wooed them to come on with the Mission, as he had done with others. Within ten weeks of their appointment, they had raised their needed support and were off to the field. The Ruegseggers had a dual appointment with CBHMS and Wycliffe Bible Translators. Both boards were needed because that was the only way missionaries could get into Mexico back in the 1950s.

The Ruegseggers worked among the Zapotec Indians translating the Bible into the Zapotec dialect in Cuixtla, 60 miles south of Oaxaca. Providing God's Word for more than 15 Zapotec communities, the Ruegseggers labored to this end for 20 years.

A detailed account of their ministry is recorded in the book, ***There Must Be an Easier Way***[1] written by their daughter, Dr. Gerry Gutierrez. ***There Must Be an Easier Way*** records in fascinating detail the life and times of the Ruegseggers. From this text we learn that CBHMS had just formed when the Ruegseggers came calling, looking for a CB-related mission with whom to work. Manis and Jane had applied with Conservative Baptist Foreign Mission Society (CBFMS), but were flatly turned down for being too old. They were 31 years of age. Back in those days, that seemed a lot older than it would be considered today! At 31, one was considered practically over-the-hill for cross-cultural endeavors. When Manis and Jane applied with the Mission, Manis had been serving as pastor of Fairview Heights CB Church in Inglewood, California, south of Los Angeles. Though turned down by the Foreign Society, they were quickly accepted by CBHMS. CBHMS leadership saw their zeal, commitment and potential for Kingdom use. It was a good fit, and CBHMS knew it.

When Manis and Jane, with their two children, arrived on the field of Mexico in February of 1951, their intent was to focus on the daunting task of breaking down the Zapotec language and translating the Greek text of the New Testament into Zapotec.

Beginning in 1951 with language acquisition, which required two years of daily stick-to-it-tive study, they were able to start the complicated New Testament translation process in 1953. All said and done, with more than their share of missionary adventures, the Ruegseggers completed the Zapotec New Testament in 1971. When Dr. Rufus Jones (CBHMS General Director at the time) and CBHMS Field Secretary Norman Wetther attended the 1971 Zapotec New Testament dedication ceremony in Mexico, they rejoiced that the evangelical churches in the many rural Zapotec communities would have God's Word in their own language. CBHMS's choice in appointing the Ruegseggers 21 years earlier had proven wise.

Those first 19 years were harrowing times for Manis and Jane. Their many stories included, for example, being pursued by a gun-wielding Catholic priest and being saved by the hands of the few evangelicals. Of course there were not many evangelicals in that area during those early years. As it would turn out, Manis and Jane's presence, coupled with the activity of other missionaries, would prove significant to the spread of truth in this region. It was common during these years and, indeed, from the late 1800s when evangelicalism first entered Central America, for evangelicals to be threatened, beaten, jailed and/or run out of town for not cooperating with the Catholics. Nearly all historical data records this as standard fare for evangelicals.[2] This has been shown from the testimony of Friends missionaries at the turn of the 1900s in eastern Guatemala to the journals of Cam Townsend[3] in Honduras in 1918 to the hidden Zapotec tribes of Southern Mexico during the 1950s, '60s, '70s and early '80s.

Those 19 years for Manis and Jane also included falling madly in love with the Mexican Zapotec sub-culture, which had been around for hundreds of years. This was a sub-culture and race of people who had been around long before Hernán Cortéz' chilling battles with the Aztecs.

The Zapotecs had been a small kingdom of Indians who, during the Dark Ages, were sandwiched between the two mighty powers of the Aztecs and Mayans. Never having been able to compete on the same powerful terms with the Aztecs, the Zapotecs collaborated in secret with Cortéz' Spanish force[4] to rid the region of the intimidating Aztecs. Being tricked themselves by the Spaniards, they remained in history as subservient to the new Spanish conquerors. They remained as slaves to the invading Europeans seeking minerals (e.g., gold, silver) and rare spices.[5] Like many of their Central American Indian cousins, many Indian tribes chose to mix in with the Spanish race. While they integrated, they still remained a very well-defined and occasionally hostile sub-culture.

Many of the Zapotecs elected to resist integration with the Spanish, which fostered their further isolation and the preservation of their culture and language. For the most part, their worldview, code of values, cultural cues, languages and behaviors were distinct. Many have stayed this way to this day. These unique and colorful Zapotec Indians were sought out by Manis and Jane in this rural setting south of Oaxaca. Manis and Jane quickly found out that, while many Zapotecs had become Catholics during the Spanish *conquistador* "Black Legend"[6] years, they had largely held onto their nature-centric religious worldviews[7] to create a syncretized Catholic/animistic form of Christianity. It was into this context and into these very rural Sierra Madre Mountains that these young and enthusiastic new missionaries drove their rickety car to begin their not-so-rickety career. They would live there until called home to Heaven. It would take such a calling to separate themselves from these beloved Zapotec Indians.

Working on the mission field rarely permits missionaries the opportunity of myopically focusing on one concentrated area of need. As we have seen, Manis was prepared for language work and completed the New Testament within two decades. With the needs so great and with workers so few, Manis and family found themselves doing medical missions as well. Manis had never been formally trained for this – another missionary field-trained Manis. Delivering Zapotec babies, stitching up wounds, treating patients for sicknesses, giving general checkups and injecting medicines became standard fare for Manis. This labor of love was carried out not only during his 19 years of translation duties, but all the way through to the early '80s. Ultimately, he would turn over his own clinic to his daughter, Gerry, who, unlike her father, had actually received formal medical training. With her husband, Gerry served the medical needs of the Zapotecs further into the mountains in Loxicha – 20 miles south from her parents' location.

Jane Ruegsegger passed away in 1982. She was with Gerry at the time, practically in her arms. Jane passed away quite suddenly in her early sixties due to an untimely stroke. Believers from neighboring communities arrived by the typical Central American truckload to serenade their lost loved one with songs, which lasted through the night. Manis wept bitterly.

Manis, though grief-stricken due to the loss of his father that same year and the closing of his clinic, lived on in Cuixtla for more than a dozen years. Though officially retiring with CBHMS in August of 1985 having completed 35 years of service, he continued in ministry in Cuixtla by focusing on leadership preparation among the Zapotec leaders amidst their fledgling, indigenous churches. He passed away in November of 1996, being laid to rest next to the love of his youth, on a hillside overlooking Cuixtla. The Zapotec communities mourned and wept his passing.

Manis and Jane's daughter, Gerry, and son-in-law, Dave, ministered in the same area on into the new millennium. With their children, Isaiah and Tava, as active co-workers, they distributed evangelistic audio-visual materials among Indian groups throughout Mexico and South America. Gerry commented, "We feel that everything we do is because of the foundation my parents laid. We are standing on their shoulders and reaching more than they ever dreamt possible."

Ruby Scott

What do midnight bandits, gospel tracts and two single women have in common?

Ruby Scott (left center) and Vi Warkentin (right center) with Tila Chol Indians.

Ruby Scott was appointed with CBHMS in 1953. The Lord wasted no time getting her to the field where she soon found herself spending ten years among the Tumbala Chols of Chiapas. She, together with her fellow single female missionary partner, Vi Warkentin, gave of herself tirelessly to assist a translation team in bringing the New Testament to the ears and hands of the Tumbala. Like the Ruegseggers, Scott was jointly appointed by CBHMS and Wycliffe. Following her years with the Tumbala, she found herself getting older. Yet – like many missionaries – she wanted another challenge, and so Ruby and Vi moved to the Tila Chol area to begin a new work.

During those first few weeks among the Tila Chols, they were serenaded by nightly violent attempts of townspeople to break into their newly-constructed wood plank home. While at night the Tila were violent, the daybreak always brought calm. While at night the missionary team determined that they would leave once and for all the next day, the daybreak brought calm and renewed perseverance.

Ruby had been prepared from her youth for opposition, having grown up in a non-Christian family and having to give herself to the Lord in secret. It had been through the testimony of Manis and Jane Ruegsegger, while at a CB Women's Missionary meeting in Yuma, Arizona, that Bible translation work gripped her heart and effectively changed her life. While having been a nurse earning a good living, she gave this up to follow in the steps of the Ruegseggers.

For several months after their arrival, these foreign, fair-skinned "women devils" – as they were called – were ostracized. Yet, as Ruby and Vi learned the language and accommodated their lifestyles to their host community, they were gradually accepted. Following two years of language study, they began with their primary goal of New Testament translation.

Recorded in her autobiography ***Jungle Harvest***,[8] Ruby records, in 125 mouth-dropping pages, the challenges that many modern missionaries do not often endure. Coupled with translation privileges, Ruby and Vi supplemented their love for the 200 Tumbala villages with church planting, medical care, ethno-musicology, Christian radio programming, counseling and basic grade-school education for children – all in the context of superstitious, machete-wielding men out with a vengeance for the missionaries and for each other.

Congregation of Tila Chol Indians gathered outside their church – 1970.

Ruby and Vi must have had lots of energy or they would never have gotten their translation work done! Indeed, they did complete the New Testament translation and many other ministries, too. Having begun in 1960, they submitted their final New Testament draft in 1974 to the Wycliffe Center in Tlalpan, Mexico City. Many missionaries had passed through these Tlalpan doors with such final drafts. It was a sad day years later in 1986 when the Mexican government made good on Wycliffe Founder Cam Townsend's 1936 promise to turn over the keys of the Wycliffe campus to the Mexican government fifty years later. While every one hoped that Uncle Cam's promise would long be forgotten, Wycliffe made good on its word and moved out. Yet, not without a few bumps in the road, such as a terrorist campus bombing in 1985 in which CB missionary Debbie O'Connor recalls first-hand with a fright, "Those terrorists did not like us!"

When asked about the cost of the simple New Testament, it was answered, "20 pesos." Yet, the cost was much more than 20 mere pesos. It amounted to a wealth of years of sacrifice by two single women, committed to being a positive influence in a negative society, in spite of the cost.

Years later, into the 1990s, the villages where these two brave women pioneered saw dramatic change. The indigenous churches are now more than 48 in number with members totaling more than 4,000. These churches are self-governing, self-leading and self-propagating. The radio programs continue unabated and additional New Testaments have been printed.

Vi would later return to Dallas, Texas to care for her aging parents and to work at the Wycliffe home office.

Ruby continued with CBHMS for many years, working with the Navajos for a while in Arizona and directing the CB released-time radio programs. She officially retired with CBHMS in the mid '80s and lived on into the next millennium in Waxhaw, North Carolina. Yet, Ruby is not one to really retire. She took the time to prepare a number of texts for the Tumbala believers in their native tongue, including a Bible concordance and an Old Testament survey. Where does she get her energy? "He makes my feet like hinds' feet and sets me upon my high places," (2 Samuel 22:34) would be Ruby's response.

Vitalino and Ester Méndez

Vitalino and his family have lived near Huehuetenango, Guatemala, since the early 1990s. Though living in Guatemala, their hearts have been in Chiapas, Mexico, where they have aggressively reached out to rural mountain Indians. They have needed to live on the Guatemala side due to the impossibility of legally obtaining residency status in Mexico.

A Look at Central American Indian Groups

Taking a deeper look at the Central American Indian groups, one finds gentle-hearted, passive people who generally live in mud huts in which rain water often passes through with each heavy storm. Their beds and hammocks are off the ground to provide a dry, peaceful sleep. The walls are of sticks or adobe and the roofs are usually of thatch. Their homes, as a whole, are usually quite dark and made up of one large living area, within which one often finds a bit of clutter – chickens running around and drying tobacco plants hanging from strings. While communities generally have running water, Indians none-the-less sponge bathe close by or bathe in the river. Like that of other peasant societies throughout the Third World and like that of their Mayan ancestors of a thousand years, Indian groups generally live off the land and live in areas where there is no electricity. It becomes obvious that outreach into their lives is a challenge, given that most missionaries come from a post-industrial/informational context. It has been within this context which many CB missionaries have compas-

Typical Central American Indian hut – 2000.

sionately attempted to effect change, extending the Kingdom amongst the poorest of the poor.

Other CB Missionaries in Mexico

- **Henry and Julia Buzo.** CBHMS appointed Henry Buzo, a Mexican national, who was originally sponsored by the First Baptist Church of Rockford, Illinois, in 1952 and took over a new work in Jalapa, near Vera Cruz, Mexico. The Buzos traveled to the interior of Mexico to evangelize portions of the department (state) of Puebla and nearby areas. They also started a church in Jalapa, but eventually left the Mission in 1968 to become self-supporting.
- **Jim and Faye Tucker** worked in Guadalajara for six years from 1962 to 1968 to establish a church, before moving to Yuma, Arizona, to work along the border, developing the CB presence there, where they continued with the mission through to the mid '90s.
- **Greg and Debbie Thayer** came on with the Mission after having spent nearly two decades in youth ministry. After a year in language school in Antigua, Guatemala (1998-99), they moved to Mazatlán, Mexico, to begin ministry.

Greg and Debbie Thayer, Daniel, Abby – 2001.

Many other CB missionaries have served the Lord under the CB banner in Mexico down through the years. A whole text could be (and should be!) written relating to the ministry of the Fountains, the Gerbers, the Gromans, the Bowmans, the Courteols and others. While some of the saints who served in Mexico are written of here, it is noted that many more triumphs and tragedies have taken place which have earned a place in history, especially with regard to the vibrant CB work along the northern Mexican border.

Final Thoughts on Mexico

As of 2000, Mexico stands as one area within Latin America with phenomenal spiritual needs. Mexico is the fourth largest Latin American country, yet has one of the smallest percentages of evangelicals.[9] Many missions, as well as our own, have recognized this, sending more than 1600 Protestant missionaries distributed among 178 sending agencies[10] to this country of 100 million people. The CBs have done a good job in their area of ministry along the northern and southern borders. Yet, the possibilities for a broader and deeper ministry are endless.

As the Mission gives thought toward expanding its imprint on the gigantic and needy face of Mexico, a thorough demographic study is called for. Demographics have always been a first or, in this case, a continuing step toward effective mission. A study relating to MTA's future role in church planting, TEE and additional missionary placement is foundational toward forward-looking ministries. Resources to kick off such a review would be, among others, Barret's ***New World Christian Encyclopedia***, MARC's ***Mission Handbook*** (published bi-annually) and Patrick Johnstone's ***Operation World***.

What would need to be considered? Here are some things to consider as a start:

1. What is happening collectively among all missions who are involved in Mexico?
2. What is happening within CB circles?
3. What are the locations of greatest need from a Kingdom perspective (i.e., the southern Baja Peninsula vs. the mainland)?
4. What are appropriate and/or optional mission strategies for MTA missionaries? For example, church planting by extension vs. the pastoral approach model (both described in this text).
5. What long-term time-table for implementation can be set into place?
6. What can we learn from the history of other CB personnel in other locations – either in Mexico, such as along the northern border, or in Central America?

Benefits to this project would be to not only keep an overall direction and vision in focus in the context of concrete data for existing missionaries in Mexico, but it would also facilitate the recruitment and direction of future missionaries.

Looking toward the future, the Mission in 2000 asked Aaron Palmatier to serve as an MTA specialist to Mexico. His role would be to monitor the existing CB work, as well as to look toward the future in terms of the many needs of this vast land.

---

[1] Gutierrez, Gerry, ***There Must Be An Easier Way***. No publisher information recorded with text, 1985.

[2] Many historical texts reveal these details, including both the personal journals of Cam Townsend as well as the historical papers of the Friends of Southern California missionaries.

[3] Steven Hugh, ed., ***A Thousand Trails***. Langley, BC, Canada: CREDO Publishing Corporation, 1984, pp. 45f.

[4] Many contemporary and historical texts relating to the Spanish conquest of the Aztecs record these details. Stephen Neill, ***A History of Christian Missions***. London: Penguin Books, 1986, p. 144: "The Aztecs, through their cruelty, had made themselves hated by the neighboring peoples, among whom the Spaniards found ready allies."

[5] Many texts document this, including Rafael Leiva Vivas, ***Tráfico de Esclavos Negros a Honduras***. Tegucigalpa, Honduras: Editorial Guaymuras, 1987.

[6] The Black Legend theory relates to attributing the Spanish Catholic rule over Latin America (1500s to 1821) with primarily relations of cruelty and vice on behalf of the Spanish crown.

[7] Nature-centric religions relate to identifying one's gods with aspects of nature – for example, the sun god, the moon god, the harvest god.

[8] Scott, Ruby, ***Jungle Harvest***. Wheaton, IL: Conservative Baptist Home Mission Society, 1988.

[9] ***Operation World*** reports 5.2 percent are evangelical as of 1993. Patrick Johnstone, ***Operation World***. Grand Rapids, MI: Zondervan, 1993, p. 379.

[10] Siewart, John A., ed., ***Mission Handbook***. Monrovia, CA: MARC Publications., 2001. This data places Mexico as the country having more expatriate missionaries and mission boards than any other country.

Guatemala –

The Republic of Indians

Otto de la Cruz of Guatemala City [11]

Having recently graduated from CAM International's Bible Seminary (SETECA) in Guatemala, Otto and Rosa de la Cruz moved to Belize to work with and be trained by Mission to the America's N.T. Dellinger. The year was 1989. Otto and his family lived in Belize for three years, whereupon they returned to Guatemala City to begin the CB work on the northeast side of the city. The vision for beginning a work in Guatemala was the joint vision of James Duren and N.T. Dellinger. Otto proved to be the Lord's vehicle whereby that vision was birthed and developed.

"It's a Vision Thing"

In the fall of 1992, Otto and his family moved to Guatemala. Otto, Rosa and their five daughters – Cicelia, Lilian, Rosa, Rut and Loida – were happy to be back in their homeland. They were "*Chapinos*" at heart wanting to reach fellow *Chapinos* (*Chapinos* are what folks in Central America call Guatemalans). Otto determined in his heart that he would win the

hearts of his fellow Guatemalans and plant churches.

Otto and Rosa de la Cruz – 1993.

Otto is a man of vision. He has a vision to walk faithfully with the Lord and a vision to work without ceasing so that others know and walk with the Lord. Effective ministry requires such vision, too. Vision relates to an impression upon one's spirit regarding a new expression of God's Kingdom that is yet to be realized. "Vision comes in the form of a 'mental portrait,' indicating this as a picture that exists in the mind's eye of the leader."[12]

Otto was such a person with a mental portrait of what he was asking the Lord to do in Guatemala. Due to this vision, coupled with hard work and the blessing of God, Otto has come to see the spiritual face of Guatemala change. The need among missionaries is to possess vision for God's Kingdom based on that which He has placed within their heart. Missionaries are challenged to look beyond the visible into the unseen world of God's desires, taking hold of one portion of God's desire to extend His Kingdom in some way.

Vision has been seen down through the years by other famous missionaries. In the 1930s Gladys Aylward, a simple parlor maid in London, became a model missionary of vision. Packaged in a tiny, frail body, this "small woman," as she was known, traveled solo across two continents to work in the Orient. This indomitable, courageous pursuit of her vision prepared her for 20 years of tireless

Otto de la Cruz's first CB church in Guatemala.

labor in the mountains of China, where she served the Chinese people in lonely, horrendous and dangerous circumstances.[13]

Mother Teresa of Calcutta was also a woman of vision. With a vision to care for the poorest of the poor in the name of the Lord, she challenged others to join her as "Missionaries of Charity." She amazed the world as her ranks of fellow sisters swelled past 4,000 as she challenged them with complete sacrifice in order to serve the destitute of this world. Mother Teresa possessed vision and yet multiplied her honorable labor by means of bringing other sisters along in her God-sent vision.

Missionaries like Aylward, Mother Teresa and Otto de la Cruz have dared to stand against the wind as they have held on to a personal vision and walked a narrow, uphill path, seeking to honor the Lord by making His name known in regions beyond their comfort zone. They have known that, "Where there is no vision, the people will perish."[14] They have known that each human has one life to live and that each missionary has only one life to give. With spiritual eyes set on the hope, "Which is an anchor to the soul" (Hebrews 6:19 NIV), missionaries like Otto de la Cruz have gone forth in the strength of the Lord as they have retained within their hearts the purpose and vision for which they were called. And passing on that vision to others, they have multiplied their co-workers in the eternal task. Guatemala and all of Central America have needed missionaries like Otto who, like William Carey, "expected great things from God and attempted great things for God."

Through the 1990s, Otto proved himself an apt church planter, planting 15 churches in six years. These are the locations listed in the order started:

- ✓ Lomas de San José
- ✓ Illusiones de Zona 18
- ✓ Vista de San Luís
- ✓ La Pasqua
- ✓ Villa Hermosa (Zone 12)

✓ Las Conchas (Zone 16)

✓ Llanos de Sta. Maria

✓ Prado de Villa Hermosas

✓ Catarina San Marcos – in the San Marcos county near the western Guatemala border of Mexico.

✓ Las Pilas – also in the San Marcos county near the western Guatemala border of Mexico.

✓ El Olvído – also in the San Marcos county near the western Guatemala border of Mexico.

✓ Prados de Villa Hermosas Roma – Zone 12 of Guatemala City

✓ Altos de Sta. Maria

✓ Residencial El Atlantico (Zone 18)

✓ La Resurreción de Las Ilusiones

Two Approaches to Church Planting

De la Cruz applies what the author of this book has termed "the pastoral approach to church planting." The pastoral approach is a church-planting model that generally envisions a new church planted by the church planter within a given time frame. It may also envision a series of individual churches planted by the church-planting missionary. It is generally the hope within this model for the new church(es) to be forever growing within its walls. The pastoral model can be an effective approach, especially when the church planter has the gifts, the desire and the energy to serve as an up-front leader for the new church(es). Otto de la Cruz is a man with lots of energy. This drive, coupled with his pastoral abilities, allows him to do quite well and, indeed, to prefer this pastoral approach to church planting. It is easily observed that most of the CB church-planting missionaries down through the years have used this pastoral approach.

A contrast can be drawn, however, between this pastoral approach and an alternative approach used in other CB areas in Central America. This contrast is not to show one model as better than the other, but rather to show that for differing geographical areas, differing spiritual giftedness factors and differing personality factors, alternative church planting models are occasionally in order.

Church planting by extension (CPE) is such an alternative approach. CPE is realized as the church planter elects not to ever function as the pastoral up-front leader, but rather proceeds to disciple mature, adult men who go on to become leaders in their respective communities, imitating the manner in which the church planter has made disciples (cf. 2 Tim 2:2). As contrasted with the pastoral approach to church planting, CPE does not require the daily presence of the missionary in the geographical location of the given new church.

The church planting by extension model envisions multiple new churches starting at once. Each church is encouraged to birth baby churches, thus establishing "chains of churches" in various geographical directions. Church growth within the extension approach is not seen merely within the four walls of the given churches, but is seen as each new church has several baby churches. Church planting by extension sees, as its goal, churches that are multiplying themselves.

It is interesting to note that, while this model is valid and effective, CB church-planting missionaries have rarely applied it. Exceptions are seen among the HEBI churches of Honduras and the HEBI-West churches of western Honduras.

Food for Thought – What factors are to be considered for a new missionary in determining which church-planting approach to use? How can we avoid the clash between those who use different models? How possible is it for different models to exist side by side or within the same mission or country?

Mike and Lisa Ratzky – Central America from 1994 to 1998

Mike and Lisa Ratzky – 1998.

Mike and Lisa spent four delightful years under MTA's Partnership Ministry. Though they lived in Tegucigalpa, Honduras, from 1994 to 1996, their happiest years were spent in Guatemala (1997-1998). While they loved this country and the rich colorful people of Guatemala, most of the year found them traveling hither and thither energetically hosting groups from the States. They tirelessly served as middlemen between folks who came from the States to serve and folks from Central America. An outgrowth of their love for Guatemalans was Mike and Lisa's decision to adopt a Guatemalan child. Mike and Lisa returned to the States with their adopted daughter in 1998.

Lillian I. Migliorini at the Christian Academy of Guatemala City

Lillian Migliorini, a single missionary, has been teaching at the Christian Academy of Guatemala City from 1995 past the turn of the 21st century. With more than 200 students, the school's primary focus is to provide a quality Christian education for "MKs" who come from over 44 U.S. and Canadian mission organizations.

Migliorini's primary focus in Guatemala has been teaching children with learning disabilities. Living out Christ's mercy and care for children is her love and calling. Because she teaches MKs, the parents are free to devote their full time to their calling, whether it's Bible translation, literacy work, or church planting. In this sense, Lillian is a missionary to missionaries.

How did Lillian arrive at this special calling? As a child, Lillian was raised by a Christian mother and attended church. She participated regularly in Sunday school, Vacation Bible School, Bible Club, Pioneer Girls Club and other church-related activities. When she was around nine years old, she committed her life to the Lord. She attended a Christian high school in Cambridge, Massachusetts and later received her B.A. in Education from Wheaton College. She also earned a Masters in Education from the University of Pittsburgh in Pennsylvania.

After teaching children for over 33 years in U.S. public schools, she found herself led to pursue a cross-cultural challenge. She applied and, to her own surprise, was accepted to teach in Guatemala under the MTA umbrella. Delightfully, she followed her instincts and has never been happier since. She has said, "My vision is not only to educate special-needs students, but to supplement what their parents are teaching them. It is a team effort with the home, school and church complementing each other." She finds it refreshing to teach children from a Christian perspective and to have the freedom to tell children that Jesus loves them and cares about them.

[11] Information within this chapter relating to Otto de la Cruz comes from interviews with Otto de la Cruz and N.T. Dellinger.

[12] Barna, George, ed., ***Leaders on Leadership***. Ventura, CA: Regal, 1997, p. 47.

[13] Burgess, Alan, ***The Small Woman***. London: Pan Books Ltd., 1957.

[14] Proverbs 29:18 KJV.

El Salvador –

The Country Named for Our Savior[15]

El Salvador is one of the smallest republics in Central America. Yet the country boasts more people per square mile than the other republics. The Christian community, too, is quite active with nearly 21 percent of Salvadoreans affiliating with evangelical churches.[16]

In 1988, long before there were CB churches in El Salvador,[17] N.T. Dellinger recorded in his CBHMS Belize Field Report that he and Joy had a visitor from El Salvador. The visitor, Sammy Navas, came for one night, but stayed for four months. Having opened their hearts and home to this young *El Salvadoreño*, N.T. and Joy saw birthed in their own hearts a desire and a commitment to begin a work in this country named after our Savior.

The Lord took Moses out of Egypt for a while. The Lord knew that Moses had to find his footing before returning to his people. Nelson Enrique Júarez was much the same. Nelson had to come out of his homeland for a time in order to meet his Savior and be trained for a return to his people. Nelson returned

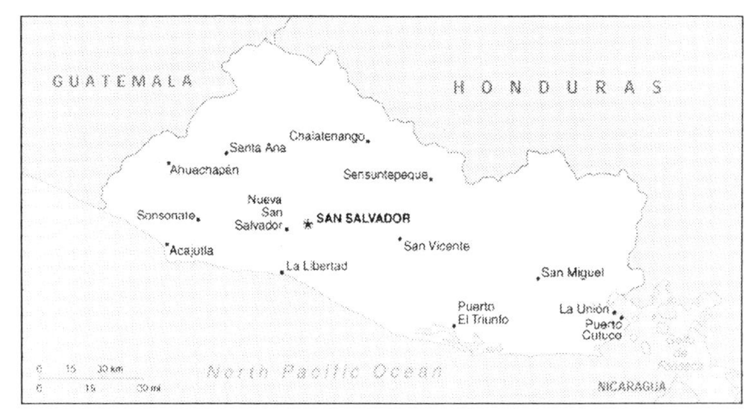

to the capital city of San Salvador, and later to Monte Karlo to begin a small group in September of 1994. His first baptized church member was an ex-soldier from the 1980s war. There were hundreds to follow. The new church would be called La Iglesia Bautista Vida Abundante.

N.T. Dellinger and Nelson Juarez – 2000.

The first public building for Nelson and his young flock was situated at 3rd Calle Oriente in Chalchuapa. This was a nice place to worship, but there was just one problem – it had no roof. It was a fine location, except when it rained.

Their next building, too, was a great edifice, except for one tiny problem – it was across from a soccer field. It was no problem Monday through Friday, but on weekends during soccer matches, the noise was overwhelming. Most churches in Central America can hold their own when it comes to loud services, but Nelson's tiny flock was no match for the competition. So they kept looking. Ultimately, they located a piece of property to buy and, with the assistance of foreign funds, a purchase was made. The CB churches of Belize sent money for the first building and the Mission's Partnership Ministries later helped build a place of worship.

Through the years, other CB churches were started. The CB church in the town of Los Cedros was started around 1997 and was later pastored by Gonzalo Bran. The CB church in the town of Porvenir came about in 1998. Partnership Ministries was instrumental in completing a beautiful building. The CB church in the town of El Refugio came into existence in 1999 under the leadership of Joel Guerrero.

During these same years, N.T. Dellinger worked by extension with Nelson to establish The Seminary of the Americas in San

Salvador[18] so as to provide training for CB pastoral leadership in El Salvador. During 1998-1999, there were more than 30 students studying in The Seminary of the Americas.

Francisco Romero was another Salvadorean who was instrumental in introducing the CBs to this tiny country. He was from Atiquizaya, El Salvador. He had been to Honduras in the mid 1990s where he met Milan Mejia, a San Pedro Sula CB church pastor. He also met MTA's Hector Newman at that time. Learning of Romero's desire to affiliate with the CBs, Paul Hutton, the newly appointed MTA Regional Specialist for Central America, and Hector Newman made no delay in visiting Romero in El Salvador. What a surprise it was to discover that two churches had already decided to affiliate with the CB banner. Thus, the work in Atiquizaya and San Salvador were to be part of the beginning of the CB work in El Salvador.

---

[15] Portions of this section were provided by N.T. Dellinger.

[16] 1993 figure taken from: Johnstone, Patrick, ***Operation World***. Grand Rapids, MI: Zondervan, 1993, p. 209.

[17] We will see in the Honduras section that CB missionary Jim Clark and his family served in El Salvador representing the CBs for a few years in the late 1970s.

[18] The El Salvador training location was an extension of the Seminary of the Americas in Belize.

Belize

The Country[19]

Formerly British Honduras,[20] this tiny English-speaking Central American nation is squeezed between Mexico and Guatemala on the Caribbean Sea. Belize is the newest nation in Central America, having gained its independence from the United Kingdom in 1981. A developing country, Belize has only four highways and 45 percent of its land is subtropical forest. It has a land area of around 14,000 square miles – about half the size of Maine – and a population of 245,000. The population is ethnically diverse and includes, in addition to the descendants of the original Mayan inhabitants of the area, various mixtures of Caucasians, Blacks, Africans, Latinos, Chinese, East Indians, Middle Easterners and Caribbean peoples living together in an environment free from racial discord. English is the official language, with Spanish being a strong second language.

Heritage of Previous Baptist Missionaries in Belize

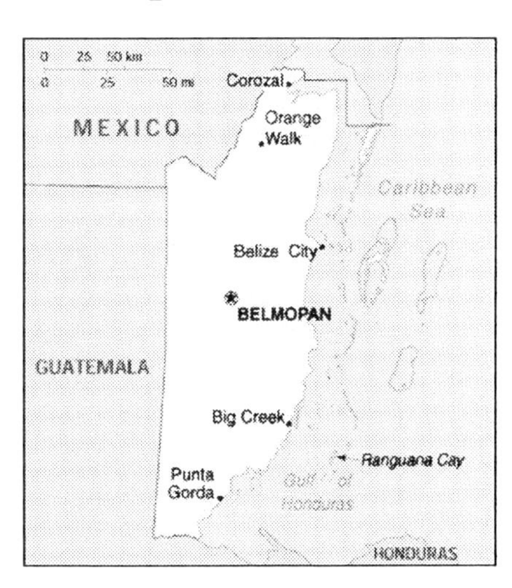

In 1822, the Baptist Missionary Society of London, England, decided to send a missionary to British Honduras. In June of that year, Mr. and Mrs. Bourne stepped off a boat to begin their ministry in British Honduras, where it was reported that "there was probably not a more wicked place under Heaven." Six months later, Mrs. Bourne was dead, largely due to the hardships of the new environment.

People with names like Henderson, Philpot, Hosken, Waring and a host of others went before us with the Good News. They became the forerunners of education. They preached the gospel to soldiers, prisoners, laborers and slaves.

In 1843, Frederick Crowe, a deacon in the Baptist Church in Belize City, sensed a call to take the gospel to Guatemala – no easy task in that day. He hired Indian men to journey with him to Guatemala, carrying 500 Bibles. He arrived in Salama, Guatemala, and gave away the first Bible to the Mayor and then attempted to sell his Bibles. These were the first known Spanish language Bibles to enter Guatemala. He held up a Bible saying, "Here I am holding a copy of the Word of God; I want to offer it for the first time for sale in Guatemala." At this precise moment an earthquake hit. God used the earthquake to make an impact on a people who believed that God was in control of nature. Crowe sowed the seeds and upwards of 30 percent of the people of Guatemala have since responded to Christ.

By 1850, the Baptist Missionary Society had withdrawn its missionaries from British Honduras and the work had largely reached an independent stage. Around this time, the Christians of British Honduras embraced missions themselves by starting a ministry on the island of Roatan, in Honduras.

In 1888, the Jamaican Baptist Missionary Society joined hands with the local Christians to do ministry in British Honduras. Many missionaries served during this time. Shortly after the turn of the century, the Jamaican Missionary Society withdrew, but left in place a prominent man who went on to invest around 50 years of his life in British Honduras among the Baptist churches – Rev. Robert Cleghorn. Cleghorn served the churches, but also the area as a whole as Mayor of Belize City. To this day, a prominent street is named after him. Through his efforts and the efforts of others, dozens of small churches were started along the Belize River. Some churches even recorded memberships of upwards of 450 people. Overall, the Baptists were growing, meeting needs and excelling in many ways.

Beginning of the CB Work

In the 1950s, Rev. Brown, a dedicated minister from England, was holding the ropes in British Honduras. He was pastoring two churches – Queen Street Baptist Church and Crooked Tree Baptist Church. He wanted to leave British Honduras, however, so he pleaded for help. Arnie Pearson and his wife were studying Spanish in Costa Rica during 1960 when Rev. Brown was pleading for help in British Honduras. The young CBHMS was still enjoying the aftermath of the miracle years of missions that had thrust the Conservative Baptist movement forward.

A local deacon in British Honduras, Robert Staine, delighted in telling the story of how CBHMS was invited to "come over and help us." Since the local group did not know what mission might come with missionary help, they invited two missions to come at the same time, thinking that they would choose one of them. The other mission (which also was baptistic) sent a missionary who stayed in a local hotel. As a result of eating local food, however, he became quite sick the night of the presentation and could not even be present. Therefore, the local group decided that the Conservative Baptists would be invited to serve their country.

In leaving language school and in coming to British Honduras to serve, Arnie commented, "We loved the people of British Honduras and praise God for good growth in lives, churches and in our family. It was a great experience and we have many fond memories." Arnie and Dorrie worked hard during that first year and led many to the feet of our Savior.

It was in 1961 that British Honduras suffered Hurricane Hattie, and the Pearsons had the job of rebuilding not only the

Queen Street Baptist Church building, but also many homes that had been partially destroyed by the hurricane. Arnie wrote at the time, "Our task was to (use Hurricane Hattie to) overcome the prejudice against the Baptist Church for its quarrelsome spirit and to rebuild the work on a more solid footing."

The Pearsons spent time on furlough in Southern California during 1962. At that time N.T. Dellinger was serving as Assistant Pastor of the First Baptist Church of Bandini in Commerce, California, and his wife Joy led the children's ministry. The Pearsons presented slides of the hurricane in British Honduras at which time the Lord sent His call to Joy and N.T. to move to British Honduras. They were appointed as missionaries with CBHMS in June 1962.

"British Honduras or Bust"

Calvary Baptist Church of Los Gatos, California, purchased a beautiful, green Jeep for the Dellingers. During their send off, a sign was placed on the truck that read, "British Honduras or bust." The Jeep was packed to the hilt with the bare essentials for living in a foreign country. After their long and tiring trek south through Mexico, they commented to each other that they were fully ready to be "uncalled" to the mission field. But after a bit of rest, their enthusiasm returned and they were quickly ready to assist the Pearsons.

N.T. and Joy Dellinger – 2000.

Throughout the '60s the Dellingers adjusted to their new home and began to reach out to others with the hope of starting new CB churches.

Ministry in the 1970s and 1980s

Ernie and Elaine Gentry served with CBHMS in British Honduras from July 1970 to 1973. Ernie ministered to many people with his special gift of mercy. They also started a primary school in Bermudian Landing.

The Belize team (left to right): Rev. N. T. Dellinger, Rev. and Mrs. Arnold Pearson, Rev. Earnest Gentry and Mr. And Mrs. Harry Bennett – 1968.

In 1970, Dick Hart worked with the Mission and had 19 students at the school at Bermudian Landing. Harry and Loretta Bennett had previously maintained the ministry there.

Throughout the '70s N.T. Dellinger served in various ways, from being a pastor to being a trainer, administrator and an all-around helper. It was during the early '70s that N.T. began to get to know Lloyd and Nancy Stanford. Lloyd Stanford would later come on with the Mission as quite a highly prized national Field Minister. It was around this time that the Baptist Extension Seminary was started to provide for leadership preparation. They also implemented a discipleship program in which all the churches used the Navigators' 2:7 program. This proved to be a great way to move disciples toward maturity.

There were three students from British Honduras attending Jamaica Bible School in 1975 when Dave Moll and his wife came to British Honduras to work with the school. The Molls served with the Mission for two years, working mostly in the area of education.

Lloyd Stanford – 1981.

The late 1970s brought harrowing times for the CB missionary team. A good friend of the missionary team, Richard, was shot and later died. Before he died, N.T. and others shared Christ with him in the hospital. He never responded as they had hoped, but instead seemed to cling to his tragic experience that had brought him to the hospital. A gunman had entered his home, killed his father and demanded that both Richard and his sister help dump the body in a well. After raping his sister and shooting Richard, the bandit finally left.

Other experiences sorely tested the missionary team, including being harassed by others – even from within their cluster of pastors – in an effort to discredit the Mission.

Jack and Edith Bernard arrived on September 26, 1980 and settled in Dangriga. Jack served the established churches in that area and also taught in the Baptist Extension Seminary. Jack and Edith had convictions that they were to live as primitively as possible. Thus, for example, they had no car – just a motorcycle.

In 1980 CB missionary Hector Newman visited Belize and surveyed the country for Spanish-speaking ministry opportunities. It was determined that the Spanish-speaking population was open to the gospel. Ultimately, this led to outreaches to Latinos and Dellinger learned Spanish in order to minister to them.

In 1981 British Honduras became what we now know as Belize. In June 1982, George Patterson visited Belize. He had been a former classmate with N.T. at Talbot Seminary. Patterson later sent one of his students, Wilfredo Hulse, to help with the Latino ministry in Belize. The missionary team had great hopes for Wilfredo as a pastor for one of the CB churches, until he decided to literally sell the congregation to another church association. Patterson wasted no time in getting back to Belize to accompany Wilfredo out of the region. Later Wilfredo was caught dealing in drugs and, though somehow still in the Honduran CB ministry as a pastor, was found guilty of drug trafficking.

Ministry during the 1980s pretty much saw church development, growth and outreach. Outreach was at a high, with Evangelism Explosion being for many years their most successful method to win people and train evangelists. N.T. Dellinger began leading seminars on evangelism, stewardship, preaching and leadership, which proved very helpful to fill some gaps for the churches. Gradually he began giving these seminars in new areas outside of Belize.

Ministry During the 1990s

Otto de la Cruz and family arrived in Belize in 1990 and, after several years of training by N.T. Dellinger, returned to Guatemala as a national Field Minister with CBHMS. N.T. discipled Nelson Júarez during the early '90s and later commissioned him to minister in El Salvador. Nelson is now a national Field Minister with the Mission.

God also kept N.T. busy with visits to San Pedro Sula, Honduras, to assist with the CB churches there. While in San Pedro Sula, N.T. found himself on the way home one night when a man pulled out a gun and screeched, "Give me all you've got." During the struggle, the would-be thief shot at N.T., but missed. N.T.'s arm was badly hurt and he lost his hearing in one ear. So when you speak with N.T., sort of aim your voice to his right ear!

The '90s were a time of growth for the Belize CB churches, with many small groups called "*Grupos de Amor en Acción*" being formed. The small groups served as a simple way to enhance relationships leading to evangelism and discipleship. While busy and blessed as ever, N.T. endured many disappointments as well. In June 1996, Santos, one of the prized workers, died of AIDS. In 1999, Pastor Jorge Lobos, a highly motivated pastor who had raised up a CB congregation of more than 60 in Orange Walk, was found to have taken funds which were not his. He tried to leave Belize in secret by plane with stolen funds, but was surprised to see

N.T. waiting for him at the airport. He pleaded for pardon, but insisted on leaving. Ever the persevering missionary, N.T. kept moving forward, in spite of others who let him down.

N.T. Dellinger's Legacy as an Example of Discipleship by Extension

As we have seen, the '90s saw N.T. reach out into new areas. In what some call "Discipleship by extension," N.T. mentored others in many areas outside of his primary geographical area. N.T.'s commitment to the Kingdom was largely responsible for opening up new locations in Guatemala, El Salvador and Honduras for the CB work. N.T. has modeled not only a pastoral approach to ministry in Belize, but also discipleship by extension outside of Belize. Completing more than 38 years with the Mission at the turn of the century, N.T. is a model for many of us in this area of New Testament discipleship by extension. Maybe that is why some call N.T. "New Testament" Dellinger.

Food for Thought – What is discipleship by extension? In what way can other missionaries employ this approach? Is it a viable approach?

Discipleship by extension extends the Kingdom of God as the wise missionary sets his eyes on a large geographical area as N.T. has and then goes about discipling faithful men in various regions of the area. As the Pauline-like missionary gives his disciples responsibility, authority and accountability, the chains of discipleship come to life. Emilio Nuñez and Bill Taylor counsel missionaries to "make disciples among us, leaving a human and reproducible legacy when you leave."[21]

There are several benefits to this approach to making disciples. First, the missionary multiplies his labor from the start in that he strategically labors in various geographical settings at one time. CB missionaries with HEBI and HEBI-West applied this approach in Honduras with good success. N.T. did so, too.

Second, discipleship by extension encourages localized leadership as ministry responsibilities rest with the disciples, not the missionaries. Since the missionary does not live in the area where the disciple is, the *extranjero* cannot assume leadership. The locals are recognized as leaders by the respective communities because the missionary is not there to create a distraction. "The true fruit of a leader is not a follower, but a new leader."[22]

This concept is illustrated with John Maxwell's diagram shown here.[23] The diagram reinforces that a missionary leader can work with one follower or many – with all accountable to him, or he can work with persons who are leaders of other fol-

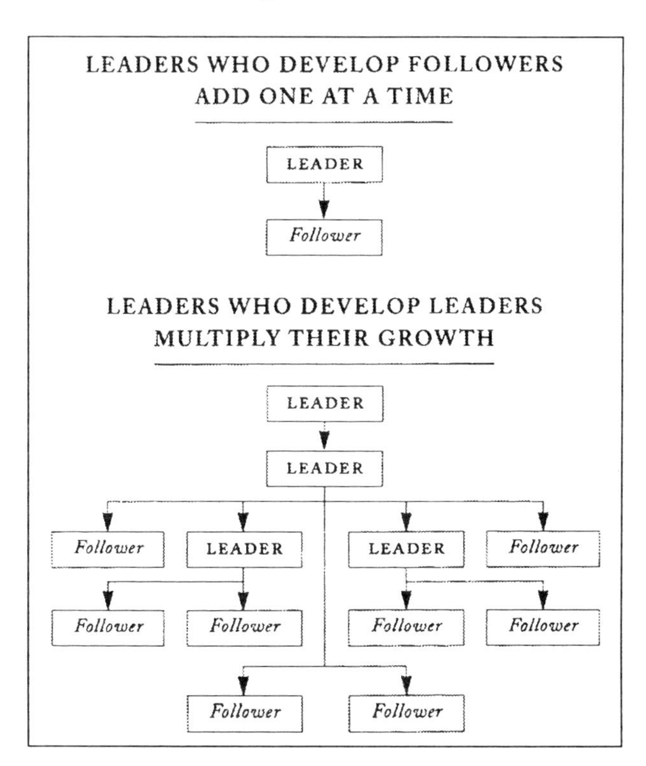

lowers. So, discipleship by extension essentially fosters the discipling of leaders and not merely followers.

Third, discipleship by extension reinforces ownership of localized ministries. It communicates from the start that each given disciple must lead his own respective area of responsibility.

Fourth, ownership leads to multiplication. As ownership of localized ministries takes place, the disciples will tend to naturally see the need to imitate their mentor's obedience in making disciples of their own. More than 100 years ago, D. L. Moody was noted for remarking that he "would rather set ten men to work than attempt to do the work of ten men."[24]

Overall, discipleship by extension brings forth localized, culturally adept leaders, not merely followers. Multiplication thus occurs.

Recapping the CB ministry in Belize, we see that during the '60s, '70s '80s and '90s, N.T. can be credited with being diligent and keeping focused on the task in Belize while at the same time substantially opening up new areas in Central America. Thinking not merely about his own "Jerusalem," N.T. established contacts and made disciples beyond his borders in Honduras, Guatemala and El Salvador.

---

[19] Information for this section of Belize was provided by N.T. Dellinger.

[20] Belize was known as British Honduras until their independence from Great Britain in the early 1980s.

[21] Nunez C., Emilio A. and William D. Taylor, ***Crisis in Latin America***. Chicago, IL: Moody Press, 1989, p. 417.

[22] Schwarz, Christian A., ***Natural Church Development***. Carol Stream, IL: ChurchSmart Resources, 1996, p. 68.

[23] Maxwell, John C., ***The 21 Irrefutable Laws of Leadership***. Nashville, TN: Thomas Nelson, Inc. 1998, p. 209.

[24] LePeau, Andrew T., ***Paths of Leadership***. Downers Grove, IL: InterVarsity Press, 1983, p. 49.

Honduras –

The True "Banana Republic"[25]

Long before the thought of a CB mission, the Lord was at work mobilizing His troops for the harvest. More than 50 years prior to the appointment of the first CB missionary to Honduras, the Lord was blazing new paths to this banana republic. Who first began the evangelical work in Honduras?

In the late 1890s, an evangelical missionary to El Salvador named Mr. Dillon found himself in Kansas City challenging an adult Sunday school class with a vision for Latin America.[26] Mr. Dillon was not only a missionary dedicated to the task, he was a man who knew where he was going. He knew his vision and he was ready to pass it on. A young Edward Bishop accepted Dillon's challenge on that day in Kansas City, and within a short time found himself on a boat to Honduras, arriving in 1896 as who many believe to be the first North American missionary to Honduras. He touched his nervous foot onto Puerto Cortés before taking a long and slow train ride to San Pedro Sula and then on to Santa Rosa de Copán in western Honduras by mule. Bishop served in Central America for nearly 50 years, passing away on the field in 1947.[27]

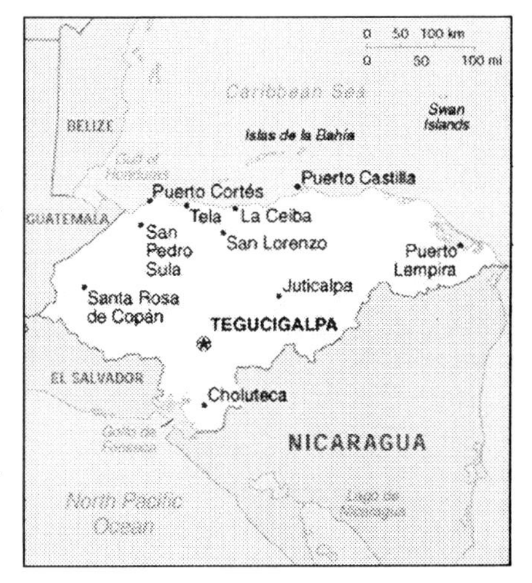

Before his home going, Bishop would play a part in the lives of the first CB missionaries to Honduras, Lee and Mildred Irons. It is interesting to note that not only did Bishop play a role in the life of CBHMS, but he also was instrumental in mobilizing the entry of other missions to the field, including the Friends Mission.

Bishop also trained and discipled a young Cam Townsend,[28] who would later found the world's second largest missionary-sending agency, Wycliffe Bible Translators. Throughout the New Testament and throughout mission history, we see this common pattern of men and women with vision mobilizing others for service. The Apostle Paul was a missionary with vision, yet he was one who passed on his vision as well. Following his third missionary journey – during his time "on furlough" in Jerusalem – Paul "began to relate one by one the things that God had done among the Gentiles through his ministry" (Acts 21:19). Paul related what the Lord was doing throughout his travels – discipling others and preparing them to carry on in the work. Men like Timothy and Titus were set into action as Paul passed on to them a vision to reach out to others beyond their cultural borders. It was through such a vision for God's harvest that CBHMS entered Honduras.

The Period of Beginnings in North Central Honduras – 1952 to 1958

La Ceiba – First Mission Efforts Under Lee Irons

Shortly after CBHMS was formed in 1950, Lee Irons and his wife Mildred, with their three children, were appointed to serve in Honduras. Lee and Mildred had been serving under CAM International for several years in Honduras. They had spent time in western Honduras in Santa Barbara, but had recently been working on the north central coast in La Ceiba since 1946.

It was during their 1951 furlough that the Ironses left CAM International in favor of a return to Honduras under the CB banner. They arrived in La Ceiba on April 24, 1952, which is considered the official beginning of CBHMS work in Honduras.

Following their appointment and having re-started in La Ceiba with the Mission, the Ironses promptly purchased a house just four blocks east of the center of the city in Barrio Potreritos. They remodeled it so that a small chapel could be constructed under their living quarters. Services were soon started after the chapel was completed. Through their efforts, the first Baptist congregation was established in La Ceiba. The church is there to this day. Lee and Mildred were well received with Lee quickly becoming known as "*Don Andrés*" to the locals.

Word Spread to Roatan Island about the Ironses

Word soon spread of the new CB missionary with the result that interested Christians began to visit the Ironses from all over the region. Christians began to invite Lee to visit their homes, churches, or ministry points along the famous Standard Fruit Company narrow-gauge rail line, which spanned nearly the entire north coast at the time.

During his north coast ministry, Irons also visited the small bay island of Roatan off the north coast of Honduras. It measures 25 by 4 miles and is one of three Honduran islands. It is populated by English-speaking Garífuna people of African descent.

The islands were visited by Columbus during his journeys to explore new lands and extend the gospel reach. European pirates, and later Great Britain, controlled the island for many years with the result that during the time of the CB ministry on the island, Roatan had long since become an English-language island.

There had been Baptist churches on the Bay Islands dating back to the mid-1800s, when Jamaican missionaries carried the gospel to these parts. In the 1900s, the foreign missionaries left the area, most likely due to the First World War. They had not adequately raised up local leadership and so, as a result, the Roatan churches suffered for years with inadequate leadership. Two key laymen on Roatan were exceptions: Mr. Carl Woods in

Coxen Hole and "Captain" Sam in Oakridge. These two men had stepped into the gap and were doing their best to hold services in churches at Oakridge, Flowers Bay and West End. They also visited and encouraged the believers in Coxen Hole, French Harbor and Sandy Bay. Additionally, this team did evangelistic work among the Garífuna people at Punta Gorda on the north side of Roatan Island, where CB missionaries would later serve – Darryl and Nadine Davis during the mid-1970s, John and Hope Miller during the 1980s and Ruth Palnick during the late 1990s. When Woods and Captain Sam heard of Lee's ministry on the mainland, they promptly invited him to visit Roatan. During his exposure trip to the island, Lee found a warm welcome and keen interest in biblical teaching, evangelism and discipleship. It would be the start of a long and healthy relationship with the Mission.

As we have seen, Roatan is, in part, made up of Garífuna people. The Garífuna people originally came from the African regions of Nigeria and Camaroon. During the reign of the Spaniards in the New World during the 1500s to 1700s, scores of Garífunas suffered the Black Legend[29] torch of slavery at the hands of *conquistadors* and others in power. The Spaniards salivated for the minerals and spices of the West Indies and Central and South America. To acquire these commodities, they went to every extreme of cruelty and cost to export black Africans from their homelands as a source of cheap labor toward their evil end. From this setting, the Garífunas were originally deposited like cargo on the island of San Vincente in the Caribbean. In 1797, due to an "enough is enough" mentality, many Garífunas fled from San Vincente to the shores of Honduras, settling in Trujillo (Colón), Triunfo de la Cruz (Atlantida) and Punta Gorda (Roatan). Since that time, they formed new waterside communities on the Caribbean shores. The Garífunas are a people of the sea. They love the food of the sea and the lifestyle that proximity to the ocean offers. They are a relational people in which tested friendships will go deep, but not broad. They love to dance and they love to fish.

The Garífunas are a people who have maintained their own culture, language, values and dress amidst a region given to change. While many Indian groups of Latin America largely adapted to the values and ways of the Spaniards, the Garífuna people generally did not. One value that many Garífunas have adopted is the "*machismo*" mentality among men. Acquired from the common *conquistador* sailor who left his wife and family in search of fortune, this value predominates much of maleness within Latin society as a whole, creating an inner drive within many men to sacrifice the love of their wives and children to "search for fortune" in the streets.[30] While the Garífuna culture is beautiful and rich with color and African tradition, the *machismo* mentality has influenced the Garífunas greatly, making them a difficult people to reach. This *machismo* mentality tends to relegate religious affairs to the women such that male leadership is oftentimes difficult to raise up. Yet, like so many other missionaries before them who were determined to step into the deep end of the challenging waters, CB missionaries like the Ironses determined to reach out to the Garífunas of Roatan Island. With these details in mind relating to English-speaking Garífunas, the CB churches on the island (nine churches in all, as of the late 1990s) are all English speaking. Years later, in 2001, a Garífuna man – Ambrosio Cordoba – would be appointed as a national CB missionary to serve in Western Honduras.

Ambrosio and Norma Cordoba – 2001.

So between the challenge of helping the new CB churches grow and develop on Roatan Island, engaging in evangelism and discipleship with the small but growing group of Spanish speaking believers on the mainland, Lee and Mildred found themselves quite involved and quite busy.

Word Spread to the Interior About the Ironses

The Standard Fruit Company had made its mark on northern Honduras. In addition to harvesting and exporting bananas, influencing politicians and destinies of whole political parties, they also built narrow-gauge railroad lines all over the north coast. These lines not only provided transportation for the important company product, but also permitted, encouraged and enhanced a money-making national public transportation system during an era when few decent dirt "roads" existed among the northern plains and mountains.

Lee and Mildred took advantage of the train lines, as did those who wanted to call on the Ironses from afar. Two such visitors made the trek to the Ironses' home from the distant village of Los Planes. In those days, it would be a trip of several hours, while today it is all of one hour by car. Mrs. Irma Budd and her younger sister, Miss Sylvia Wright, took the Standard Fruit train into La Ceiba to get to know firsthand the new CB missionary. Los Planes was a railroad servicing point on the Standard Fruit Company line to Coyoles Central and, for this reason, it was in a good location. It was on the southeast side of Olanchito and was a central processing location for the Fruit Company. God had given Mrs. Budd a deep burden for the children and families of fruit company workers living in Los Planes and nearby Trovatore. Mrs. Budd had responded to God's burden by starting children's classes in her home. Many adults were attending as well, drawn by the singing, flannelgraph lessons and gospel presentations. Mrs. Budd and Sylvia asked Lee to visit their home and help them expand their ministry, especially by giving Bible teaching, training young people and preparing some new believers for baptism. Lee agreed and thus the Mission's thrust into the interior was born in the early 1950s. The heart of the CB movement exists there to this day.

An Early Departure by the Ironses

In 1954 the Ironses were forced to leave Honduras because of Mildred's poor health. In spite of being close to La Ceiba's famous D'Antoni Hospital and a carefully monitored diet in this "modern" coastal town (as compared to their previous location of rural Santa Barbara in western Honduras), the ravages of intestinal parasites and malaria had taken their toll both on Lee and Mildred. As early as the spring of 1953, they felt forced to inform the board of CBHMS that they needed to return home as soon as possible. After returning to the States for a time, Lee and Mildred later returned to cross-cultural work with the Mission in Mexico. They worked both in the area of Naco and Cananea in the department of Sonora, near the U.S. border, as well as in Nogales of Sonora with the newly formed Mexican Bible Institute.[31] In light of the Ironses' departure from Honduras, Dr. Rufus Jones – who was the the mission director at the time – immediately began searching for someone to replace them.

Food for Thought – It is interesting to note that often when a North American missionary needs to leave the field, other North Americans (as opposed to nationals from the field) are searched for as replacements.[32] In the 1980s and 1990s the CBs broke this trend by actively raising up nationals as on-the-field replacements for North American missionaries. Way to go, CBs!

The Ironses had done a lot during their short tenure with CBHMS on the north coast. Notably, they won and discipled quite a number of young people. Included in this group was Walter Bush (who later served with Baptist Mid-Missions), Mary Patterson, Rex Harrison, his sister Ida and the Zelaya girls – Zoila and Zonia. Zoila later became the wife of a pastor and leader with the United Brethren in Christ churches in Honduras,

José Ramirez. The foundation laid in these young people proved to be the backbone of the La Ceiba church and the spark that was fanned into a flame that ignited many other young people to give their lives to Christ and move into effective service.

David and Marian Jones are Recruited for Service

In late May of 1953, the same board member, Claude Moffitt, who had recruited the Ruegseggers for southern Mexico, approached David and Marian Jones regarding the need to replace the Ironses. The Joneses had just resigned from the newly-formed Hindustan Bible Institute in Los Angeles and were invited to join CBHMS in Honduras. Moffitt spoke to David about the need and vision of the Mission for a Bible school to be established in Honduras, and this caught David's attention. So he and Marian prayed earnestly about this call, finally coming to a decision to apply to the Mission that summer. They were accepted in September of 1953 and went to the field with their three small children in May of 1954 to relieve the Ironses.

David and Marian Jones – 1978.

David and Marian's long tenure as missionaries began with a difficult situation. Only five days were available between the time of arrival of this English-only, wet-behind-the-ears, new *gringo* missionary couple and the departure date of the Ironses! These five days of introduction to life on the field were overwhelming. Yet, the new missionaries endured and went on to be effective career missionaries. Forty-six years later, David and Marian would look back over the vast CB work all over Central America and reflect upon their humble beginnings in La Ceiba. David would comment to this writer, "I often wonder how God could have used our feeble efforts those years ago to produce anything lasting, but, praise to His Name, He has done so! As

Paul wrote the Corinthians, 'I planted, Apollos watered, but God gave the increase.' The Spirit seems to need and use a wide variety of us frail humans to do His incredible and amazing work."

Food for Thought – What sort of introduction to the field should new missionaries be given? A trend is seen from the Ruegseggers to the Ironses to new missionaries at the turn of the new millennium that on-the-field training and orientation for new missionaries has left much to be desired. What role does this play toward attrition or unnecessary conflict?

This eye-opening week included taking care of a myriad of last minute details for Lee and Mildred's departure, leading a funeral service, adjusting to the 100 degree tropical heat and humidity, living in a noisy hotel (Hotel Paris off the central park which operates to this day) and enduring the new sounds of seemingly hourly banana trains leaving from the Standard Fruit Company station across from the hotel.

Don Andrés, as Lee was called, and David were able to take a ride on the dusty roads in and around this small coastal city in Lee's station wagon to give David an introduction to ministry. Lee's rickety station wagon was quite well known by the locals – mostly in that Lee retrieved many local children each Sunday from all over La Ceiba to transport them to church service. The locals knew this well-liked car as "*Ancho y Ondo*," taken from the chorus *Don Andrés* had taught them: "Deep and Wide" or "*Ancho y Ondo*." The car, of course, was one of those deep and wide station wagons from that era.

The Jones family came to La Ceiba, also known to many as "the pearl of Honduras," with no household goods, appliances, extra clothing, or car. Like many new missionaries to the field, they made do with what they brought in their suitcases. They learned what it meant to live on the goodwill and generosity of local believers and they would later testify of the wonderful ways in which God used nationals to help them bond with the local people. Because of limited means, they had to borrow dishes, pots, pans, kitchenware, sheets, towels and other items just to set up their new home. The local believers proved to be generous and loving, even bringing food to their door during the first month of the Joneses' arrival. While this experience was challenging, this time vitally assisted the Joneses to bond with the nationals for years to come.

Food for Thought – What can new missionaries do to bond with the nationals? How can the new missionaries bond with the host culture? To what degree does this bonding determine the effectiveness of the missionary's interpersonal relationships?

In terms of ministry, one of David's first ministry assignments was to assume the pastorate of the CB church in La Ceiba that Lee Irons had established. As it would turn out, this church would be pastored by many North Americans for years to come. As we shall see, this is often a precedent established by North American missionaries. While not being critical of the missionary customs in place at the time, this approach can be shown to stifle local leadership in the long run. Oftentimes the thought is that the missionary is the most suitable person for the pastorate. "Missionaries often say, 'When the national is mature and ready, then he can lead the work.' But he will never be mature, compared to the missionary!"[33]

While Jones had recently studied Roland Allen's books[34] and other similar literature on the importance of starting indigenous churches on the field, he was unable to find suitable nationals to pastor the church. As a result, this created an unspoken mentality within the church that only North Americans could properly pastor the church. In the early 1990s when this same church needed a new pastor, they looked for and found a North American from Florida who would come to La Ceiba to serve as a pastor. Today's approach to ministry often forms tomorrow's precedent. Lee and David's decision to function as the primary pastor, while fine at the time due to a lack of local leadership replacements, formed an enduring precedent. This is not to criticize our CB missionaries, as they sought to apply the pastoral approach in caring for God's flock entrusted to them. It is to say that oftentimes this approach is not ideal for the expatriate missionary. It can be quite effective, as we have seen earlier with Otto de la Cruz of Guatemala, as nationals minister among their own people.

During these first few months on the field, the Joneses were encouraged with a visit from a Mission Aviation Fellowship (MAF) pilot who invited this young, eager-for-fellowship couple to the ongoing Inter-Mission Committee Conference in San Pedro Sula. At the time, San Pedro Sula was quite a trek away, only being accessible by plane or a series of ferry rides across such deep and wide rivers as the Chamelicon outside San Pedro Sula.

The Joneses saw fruit for their labors in La Ceiba as well as in Los Planes, Trovatore and also on Roatan Island. Ministry in these locations led to growth in the faith and numbers of the CB congregations along the coast and on the island. Ministry also led to a first-ever CB youth conference on the island in 1955. While ministry proceeded well, the Joneses had not faired well with learning Spanish. Realizing this need, they elected to take a year of language studies in Costa Rica.

The Perrys Arrive for Service

Another new CB missionary family arrived in Honduras that year: the Oliver Perry family. The Perrys would serve as new team members in La Ceiba and would begin their CB career by following up the ministry that the Ironses and the Joneses had begun on the mainland and among the Garífunas on Roatan Island. Short-term Bible seminars were also a main thrust for Oliver Perry, which proved to raise up several pastors and workers for the CB work. Glen Solomon, the eventual key man among Roatan Baptist churches for many years – even to the end of the century – was among the seminar students.

When the Joneses needed to be gone for a year of language study, Oliver followed standard operating procedure by both assuming the pastoral duties at the La Ceiba First Baptist Church as well as supervising the work at Los Planes, Trovatore and on the island of Roatan.

Realizing that the growing La Ceiba church would soon become too large for the chapel under the mission house, Oliver, with the approval of the deacons and congregation, arranged for the mission house to be moved to the back of the property and began construction on a new and much larger sanctuary in the front of the lot. This was a great challenge for the congregation, but they rose to the occasion; with help from CBHMS, the construction moved ahead. The church building was built in 1958 on the previously-purchased Barrio Potreritos lot in the *centro* of La Ceiba – a block from the famous central park. The building is there to this day with an active congregation. Walter Bush, the young man referred to previously whom David Jones had discipled, became the pastor of the La Ceiba church in January of 1958. The pastoral baton was passed to a national! Bush carried on the services mainly in English, but also used some Spanish for the large Spanish majority of the La Ceiba population. Though he later left the church, Bush's relatives would continue on in active lay leadership through to the turn of the century.

The Ministry on Roatan Island Develops

When Glen Solomon, a Roatan islander, graduated from the residential Bible Institute at Olanchito and returned to Roatan, he found himself involved with the CB work there. Under his leadership and from meager beginnings, the work grew and flourished. Soon there would be CB churches in Oak Ridge, Diamond Rock, Punta Gorda, French Harbor, Roatan City (later renamed Coxen Hole), Flowers Bay and West End. There would also be a new church on Guanaja, the neighboring island to the east.

The Solomon family – 1977.

Solomon became a Field Minister under CBHMS and acquired a support base from U.S. churches. The vision of Glen Solomon for both new churches as well as community involvement led to the establishment of a primary school at Oak Ridge and a children's home and clinic at Gravel Bay. It also later led to a building for the Roatan Bible Institute dedicated in 1988 and a radio station. The radio station's initials were HRGS, with the "GS" referring to Glen Solomon. He led the churches for more than 35 years.

Coxen Hole CB church – 1985.

The Aguan Valley Ministry Begins

While the Perrys enjoyed ministries left in good order by the Joneses and Ironses, they had their sights on a new area as well. Oliver began taking trips to the Aguan River Valley area – where Olanchito is located. Olanchito is 22 air miles south of La Ceiba, where Perry determined that the only evangelistic efforts in the whole area had been carried on by one Plymouth Brethren man. Evangelical and Reformed Mission missionaries had also visited the area a few times, but were unable to carry on the work. Few evangelical churches existed in the area and fewer still were the missionaries who worked in that especially hot area of central Honduras. Thus, all of the parties involved welcomed Perry and CBHMS into the valley.

Being encouraged with the hope of a fruitful ministry, Oliver immediately began planning for a faith-stretching move to Olanchito. The family would relocate as soon as he could rent a house, make the necessary improvements for the comfort and well being of his family and arrange for their furniture to be crafted by local carpenters in Olanchito. He made several trips to Olanchito on the famous "*El Rápido*" train to take care of these many preliminary matters. This fast-moving, open-air train required only a five-hour ride for the 75-mile run to Olanchito from La Ceiba instead of the normal, rickety ride of 10 to 12 hours on the "*El Local*." The Perrys were quite encouraged with the hope of a fruitful ministry in Olanchito. So, within a few months they moved there.

Once the Perrys moved to Olanchito, they began evangelizing both in that city and in a number of towns and villages up into the valley, including San José, Las Flores, Arenal, Santa Barbara and San Lorenzo. God used the Perrys to disciple a number of key young men whom he had brought to Christ in the Aguan Valley. These young men would become the first class of the Bible Institute at Olanchito, which would later be started in the Aguan Valley. But with both the pastoral responsibilities of La Ceiba still on his plate as well as that of the Los Planes and Roatan churches, Oliver could not develop the work in Olanchito as he would have liked. As a result, this heavy task was left to David and Marian Jones who returned from language school and furlough in September of 1957.

The Perrys went on furlough in the fall of 1957, and the Joneses moved into their house in Olanchito. Evangelistic efforts among friends and neighbors there were blessed by God. After a series of evangelistic meetings in a rented storefront building near the *centro* in Olanchito, a small congregation of around ten new believers began regular meetings early in 1958. Following the precedent, David Jones pastored the new work. Visits to the preaching points that Oliver had started earlier were likewise continued, and Christians were encouraged and discipled, with additional converts added. By the time the Perrys returned from their furlough in September of 1958, the small congregation in Olanchito was thriving and many small groups of believers and inquirers up into the valley were active in regular gatherings for worship and witness. Indeed, God was active during these years!

Starting of the Bible Institute at Olanchito

As early as 1954, Oliver Perry had conceived of a Bible Institute program for the Honduran field. After his return to Olanchito in the fall of 1958, he continued visits to various parts of the Aguan Valley with this vision in mind. Taking the gospel to quite a few rural villages, Perry experienced a bit of opposition from Catholics as was common during those early years.[35] He was determined, though, and in due time saw many young men make decisions for Christ. Perry felt that these men could be extracted from their communities so as to be taught and trained in Olanchito, miles away. For this reason, in March of 1959, he began formally teaching two young men, José Ramirez and Juan Aguilar. Later that year, other students came into the new institute. A young Miss Silvia Wright also came to help in the teaching of Christian Education and the Bible. Classes took place at the rented chapel in Olanchito. The Bible Institute at Olanchito was off the ground.

Oliver Perry (left) at the Bible Institute at Olanchito – 1964.

Twenty students were enrolled during the 1961 spring trimester at the institute. Several students were from the United

Brethren Mission of La Ceiba. The institute needed more adequate rooms for classroom, dormitory and dining facilities. During the spring of 1961, Oliver Perry was able to get funds from CBHMS to build three structures on a parcel of land that had been purchased one kilometer north of Olanchito. The new institute buildings consisted of a classroom and library building, a men's dormitory and a kitchen/dining room.

Students of the Bible Institute at Olanchito – 1963.

The Period of Expansion into New Areas – 1959 to 1969

First Graduates – December, 1961

Although the enrollment dropped significantly during the 1961 school year, five men graduated from the Olanchito Bible Institute in December. The five young men had finished a three-year course of study. The field conference of CBHMS missionaries voted to grant each man a $100 loan to help them begin a trade while they carried on pastoral ministry. One of the men, José Ramirez, was assigned to the church in Los Planes. After many years of waiting, the Los Planes church rejoiced to finally have their own national pastor.

Meanwhile, new works began at several places in the Aguan Valley during 1961-1964. Coyoles Central started services in a local Christian's home in 1962 and later was organized when a simple wooden chapel was erected in 1964. Oliver Perry and students also made frequent visits to Jocón, a lumbering town in the mountains forty miles from Olanchito, with the hope for a new work. A church would later be started here, though with the result that once a building was provided to the church with mission funds, the church elected (a week after the church building was completed) to "jump ship" in favor of another mission. When the Los Planes settlement was removed by the Standard Fruit Company, members from the Los Planes church started a new work in Isleta Central, a nearby banana camp. This church with four others (though not the Los Planes church) later also elected to affiliate with another mission.

The Clarks Arrive in Olanchito

The Bible Institute at Olanchito added another missionary teacher when Jim Clark arrived on the field from language school in August, 1960. He had fallen madly, head over heels in love with and quickly became engaged to Hazel Winne while in language school. They wasted no time and were married in February, 1961 in the States. The Clarks then moved to Olanchito to help out with the Bible Institute. The Clarks would later move to Tegucigalpa for ministry with the Mission there.

Jim Clark (left) with graduates of the Bible Institute at Olanchito – 1966.

Radio Station HRVC Launched in Tegucigalpa

Oliver Perry was a man of energy and vision. While busy on the north coast and in the Aguan Valley, he also had thoughts during these years of a new ministry in Tegucigalpa. For several years, Perry had been chatting off and on with Howard Erickson.[36] At that time the Ericksons were serving with CBHMS at the HOXO radio station in Panamá. A plan was made to ask the Lord to permit the launching of a CB-related radio station in Honduras. Various locations were considered, including Olanchito and San Pedro Sula. After much prayer, Tegucigalpa was chosen. One influential factor was David Jones's desire to move to the Honduran capital to head up the project. After prayer and planning, the Joneses resettled in Tegucigalpa in February of 1959.

HRVC building in Tegucigalpa – 1981.

El Hatillo, on the mountain just outside Tegucigalpa, was chosen for the first transmitter and studio of HRVC. The studio motto would be "The Evangelical Voice of Honduras." At the Joneses' urging, Howard Erickson came from Panamá to install the first transmitter, a 1,000-watt, long-wave unit. The first radio programs began on December 8, 1960, with programs transmitted during four hours every evening. Somewhat later, the men obtained property at Los Guayacanes, six kilometers outside of Tegucigalpa, for a permanent transmitter and antenna tower. Eventually it was possible to erect a transmitter building at the new site. The Conservative Baptist Youth Association of Oregon purchased a 200-foot tower for the station[37] for this new ministry and HRVC would later begin its first short-wave broadcasts in 1965 with the installation of the new transmitter. In June of 1965, the studios were moved to Third Street in Comayagüela. In the late 1980s under the helm of CBHMS missionary Hector Newman, the station would again be relocated to Colonia Las Americas.

While in Tegucigalpa, the Joneses wasted no time in looking around for a place to start a new church. It was their desire not to merely facilitate the radio ministry, but to respond to God's Great Commission by always being ready to evangelize, disciple and congregationalize, though busy with other pursuits (e.g., the radio ministry). In September, 1961, David Jones began working in Colonia Sagastume, a settlement on the northern outskirts of

Tegucigalpa. They saw a small group emerge and eventually organized a church.

Then in late 1963 and early 1964, the Evangelical Alliance of Honduras invited the Latin American Mission to hold Evangelism-in-Depth in Honduras. Our Mission cooperated with the result that our missionaries found the lay training quite helpful, especially to the Sagastume work. Overall, we see that God was active in every CB endeavor. It was a period of growth and stability.

A Honduras National CB Association

In 1964 the first draft of the Conservative Baptist Association of Honduras Constitution and Bylaws was prepared by Oliver Perry. It was a re-working of the Central American Mission Association Constitution and Bylaws. The CB churches and the CB institutions (radio station and Bible Institute) were to become members of the new association. While some strong Presbyterian-type hierarchical authority was evident in the constitution and by-laws,[38] it was none-the-less ratified with Olanchito being the central site for the association office.

Meanwhile, Back in La Ceiba

After several years of Spanish ministry, the La Ceiba church began English services on Sunday mornings during October, 1964. A preacher from Roatan conducted these services, while Silvio Sanchez, one of the first Bible Institute graduates, functioned as a principal leader. Later, the English group came under the direction of Mr. Verl Owen, the former manager of the Standard Fruit Company creamery in La Ceiba. Along with his second wife, Ada, Owen plunged into the English ministry to begin another church. The new church met within the same building used by the Spanish-speaking church. Two churches (Spanish and English) meeting in the same church building created a situation that the Mission and missionaries found difficult to deal with. This was complicated by both the dynamics of a sub-culture clash as well as the resistance by both parties to be fully merged with the other organizationally. Peace was generally maintained through the years until, in the mid-1990s, tensions re-emerged. Ever the fine arbitrator, Paul Hutton (CBHMS Central America Regional Director at the time) attempted, but was unable, to reconcile the two sides. The English church voted to relocate so as to deal peacefully with the conflict. This took place during the pastoral years of Dennis Hendrickson, an American pastor and missionary. Ultimately, the English church bought property of their own in Barrio Bella Vista, a few miles south of downtown La Ceiba. Sensing a frustration that the Mission would not simply write out a blank check for assistance with construction costs, the English church elected to affiliate with the Southern Baptists soon after their move.

Issues of Field Organization

During the 1960s, ministry was thriving. As we have seen, the work on all fronts was expanding. Jim Clark had begun to direct the Bible Institute, and under his leadership the school started a creative one-year layworkers' course for young men who might only qualify for limited-time studies. Meanwhile, Oliver Perry continued aggressively to visit works and workers on the field. During 1965 and 1966, the missionaries from Olanchito and Tegucigalpa discussed at great length their total field organization and program. They saw that to reach their goals to evangelize, disciple and congregationalize, they needed to make changes in overall church development procedures, the Olanchito training program and in the Tegucigalpa radio ministry. As a result, early in 1966 Dick Falconer flew in from Wheaton to hold a conference with the missionaries regarding overall field organization. Together they agreed that the Honduras ministry would be put under three coordinators – a plan that the CBHMS board ratified later that year. David Jones would coordinate the radio ministry, Oliver Perry would monitor overall field work and Jim Clark would focus on leadership training. While these were progressive steps, the Honduran work would soon enter a new stage.

New Developments – The Extension Bible Institute Program Begins

As part of his focus on leadership training, Jim Clark attended a workshop on Bible institutes in Guatemala City in July, 1966. While there, he came into contact with the U.S. Center for World Missions founder, Ralph Winter. Winter and others from the Presbyterian Mission had started the theological education by extension (TEE) seminary program in Guatemala the year before. It was a radical new model for leadership training that fascinated Clark, and for which he would soon submit a proposal to CBHMS about how he felt the plan should be adapted to the Honduras field.

It was during this crucial period in Mission history that George and Denny Patterson arrived in Olanchito from language school in August, 1966, to begin serving on the field. Jim invited George to assist him in drafting a plan for revising the residential Bible Institute. Jim knew that Patterson's *modus operandi* was fast, and as a result, a preliminary plan was drawn up within a few months.

In October, 1966, while the Perrys were on furlough, a missionary field conference was held in Tegucigalpa. Jones, Patterson, Hutton (Paul) and Clark met and passed a resolution to close the Bible Institute at Olanchito. What was proposed was a closure of the residential program so that an extension ministry could begin. The plan called for prompt action and the new extension ministry began in January of 1967.

Because there were few usable materials available for the distinct rural nature of the leaders in the Aguan Valley, George Patterson went to work preparing simple, user-friendly, pocket-sized pastoral booklets. He wrote basic courses, which were immediately received with overwhelming applause by locals who were starved for culturally sensitive, readable, pastoral training materials. At first, the new extension ministry involved "extension centers" which the two missionary teachers would visit every week or so to hold "teaching times." There the students enrolled from the nearby churches without having to leave their place of ministry to live in Olanchito. It was ingenious. "Why hadn't anyone thought of this before?" they wondered. The students would study on their own turf and in their own homes between the weekly meetings. The materials would be discussed at the following meeting with practical homework being accounted for. Each student was to be actively engaged in some practical work, especially evangelism and church planting. With each lesson, the student was required to put his newly-learned material to work in his practical assignment, ideally in terms of teaching others what he had learned. Thus from the start, the extension plan emphasized passing on to others what was learned. Years later, Patterson was to fully develop this concept of "obedience-oriented" theological education, for which leaders from around the world would recognize him as an ingenious pioneer. Extension centers were begun all over the Aguan Valley: in Isletas, Olanchito, Campo Cuatro and as far away as Jocón.

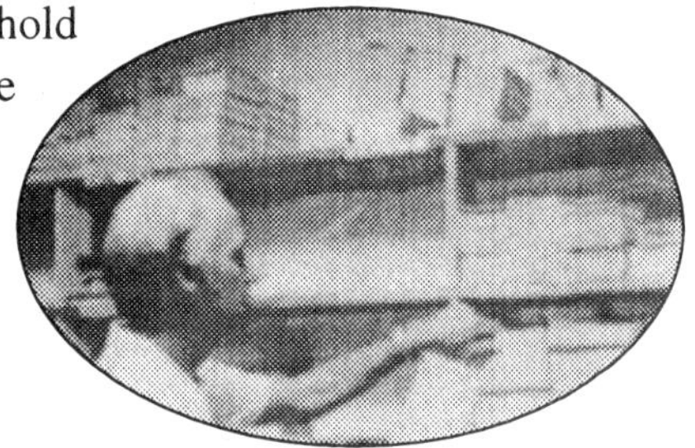

George Patterson organizing lesson booklets for extension workers – 1977.

The extension principle at work. George Patterson (left) teaches the man next to him, who teaches the man next to him, who teaches the man next to him and so on – 1977.

Clark and Patterson were happy with the extension program. They were pleased to see that the extension concept realistically adapted to the culture and lifestyle of the folks in rural

Honduras. They saw that while the residential institute had strengths as a school in itself, residential programs in general tend to struggle to enroll good pastoral candidates (i.e., mature, male adults as opposed to young, unmarried boys). They felt that the students who had graduated previously did not go back into the interior villages from which they came and which comprised a large part of the CBHMS field. Clark and Patterson took a bit of flack from others for this radical new form of ministry, but through the years, this new approach proved to show great and God-honoring results, both in this area as well as in other new pioneer areas such as western Honduras.

In June 1967, the Clarks left Olanchito for a furlough in the States. George and Denny Patterson continued there alone with the ever-blossoming extension program. While in the States, Jim Clark met with Oliver Perry at the CBHMS office in Wheaton to talk about their ministries in Honduras. It was agreed that the Clarks would move to Tegucigalpa in 1968 to assist David Jones with a new Miraflores church plant and that the Perrys would relocate from Olanchito to La Ceiba, so as to church plant near Tela. As it would turn out, the Perrys spent only a short time in La Ceiba before relocating to Puerto Rico.

Beginning of the Miraflores Work in Tegucigalpa

When the Joneses began their furlough in July of 1967, Ron Young and his wife, Joyce, came from language school to Tegucigalpa to help at HRVC and aid the Sagastume church. They also assisted with the church plant in Miraflores, for which they would later organize and lead the Sunday meetings. The Clarks would soon return from furlough in 1968 to plunge into the Miraflores church plant. The Clarks saw growth and the church was organized with 17 charter members in 1969.

Howard Erickson Becomes Manager of HRVC – 1967

Howard and Cally Erickson.

Late in 1967, Howard and Cally Erickson and their children transferred to Honduras from Panamá to take over the management of HRVC. Operation of HRVC continued to improve with additional announcers and a program director. The Ericksons would set the pace for dramatic ongoing improvements, which took place during their time in Tegucigalpa and also for the next 30 years.

The Fountains in Tegucigalpa

During 1969, Thomas Fountain, who liked to be called "*Tomás de la Fuente*" in Spanish, and his wife, Iona, arrived in Tegucigalpa. Tom had already been working since 1957 in Mexico with the Mission as a publisher of Spanish Christian literature in Mexico City before moving to Honduras. *Tomás* began the first literacy program used by CBHMS in Honduras with what was known as the Laubach method. As a vehicle toward outreach, he used HRVC and called the literacy office "Canal A.B.C." Hundreds responded to the literacy lessons by radio. A special effort was soon launched among the North Coast churches as well and eventually into the department of Olancho. Many accepted Christ through this ministry. Tom also began the preparation of literature for beginning readers, geared especially to rural populations. Some of his material was also used by Patterson and the Extension Bible Institute.

The Fountains would later return to the States in 1973, but would continue making trips to Tegucigalpa twice yearly, maintaining a literacy office with a secretary at HRVC in Tegucigalpa through the years.

The Period of Significant New Church Growth – 1970 to the 1980s

The Miraflores Church in Tegucigalpa

By 1970, Tegucigalpa had a fully established CB church in Colonia Miraflores with a new building dedicated in February of 1970. Jim Clark continued as the pastor of the group for a while. In April of 1971, the Luis Palau Crusade in Tegucigalpa provided strong added impetus to the Miraflores work and a large percentage of the evangelical churches and missions in Tegucigalpa backed the Palau Crusade.

In September of 1971, the Miraflores church called a young Honduran man as pastor who had just graduated from the United Baptist Seminary of Mexico City. He was Tency Reneau, an enthusiastic single man who had studied psychology and related areas at the seminary, but who had very little Bible training. When Reneau moved into Miraflores, the Clarks moved to another area of Tegucigalpa, Colonia Satélite.

During the second year of Reneau's pastorate (1972), serious problems arose. Lay leaders began to associate with various "big P" Pentecostal churches and attempted to persuade all of the church members to experience tongues associated with the day of Pentecost in the New Testament. Pastor Reneau found himself powerless to handle the situation because, not having been trained satisfactorily in the Bible, he could not present solid Bible teaching on the subject. Reneau felt he needed to resign with Jim Clark assuming pastoral leadership again. Once order was re-established, a good portion of the church body felt it necessary to leave to start a new non-baptistic church.

The Satélite Church in Tegucigalpa

The work at Colonia Satélite in Tegucigalpa started on Saint Patrick's Day, March 17, 1974, with Sunday morning Bible studies in the Clarks' home. During the next few months, further contacts resulted in a regular study group, including children's classes. By the beginning of 1975, the new group at Satélite was able to call René Madrid to become their pastor with 27 charter members for the new CB church. René came from San Pedro Sula, where he had planted San Pedro Sula's first CB church, as we shall see later.

HRVC in Tegucigalpa

Paul and Janie Hutton – 1999.

In 1970 Paul and Janie Hutton came back to Tegucigalpa to work with HRVC following a time in the States. Paul had done some technical work at the station in 1966 and 1967 and now returned to be the HRVC engineer during the 1970s. Paul would later manage the station, taking the baton in the spring of 1974 from Howard Erickson who retired. The vision was to move the station through a second phase of growth and then turn it over to national leadership. There were many goals: higher power for the AM transmitter, the first FM stereo broadcasts, news via teletype, literacy through radio, purchase and remodeling of the Comayagüela studio building and the writing of the new bylaws. The Lord used Paul greatly during this time, and in 1976 he was able to turn over the manager's job to a national, Felipe Aguilar. The Huttons left Honduras for a 16-year hiatus in Hawaii as, among many hats worn, Vice President of Administration for the CB-related International College. Later, in 1993, Paul and Janie would return to service in Central America with Paul serving as a Regional Specialist overseeing the ministry of nearly 30 missionaries in Central America. During his shift at the helm, the number of CB missionary families in Central America blossomed to its highest ever. Paul would continue with this role into the new millennium. Paul's easy candid-to-a-fault approach to situations proved a stabilizing force for the CB movement in Central America.

The HEBI Program on the North Coast

In north central Honduras, the extension program expanded into new areas of the Aguan Valley and beyond. The Jocón district started a chain of churches and new works began in the lower Aguan Valley. Considerable opposition came from the churches at Coyoles and Isletas who were not turned on to extension ministries, but who preferred a traditional approach to ministry. These two churches, as mentioned earlier, led three others in a decision to separate themselves from cooperation with the CBs. None of this opposition stopped the dramatic growth of the extension program. Much of the reason for this advance was the emphasis on "extension chains." When one church was established in a town or village, it would seek to reproduce itself by starting daughter churches elsewhere. Daughter churches would then start granddaughter churches.

The extension program was not so much a decentralized theological approach to pastoral training as much as it was a way to evangelize, disciple and congregationalize greater numbers of people. Each student enrolled in the Extension Bible Institute was engaged in action and not merely in passive learning procedures. Eventually, the thrust reached into the huge central department of Olancho, south of Olanchito. At first, Patterson and his student-workers had to literally walk for several days to places like Guata, but eventually Mission Aviation Fellowship planes were used to carry them to small landing strips between the mountains. Patterson insisted on going to hard-to-get-to places that were less-reached. Many new chains of churches were birthed as a result.

George Patterson (second from left, back row) with Honduran pastors and teachers – mid '70s.

What made the studies well-received was not simply the approach (i.e., the teachers and missionaries traveling to the students' villages instead of vice-versa), but also the actual material developed. Patterson developed studies better fitted to the educational level of the average men in the villages, most of whom had little elementary education. He prepared lessons on many aspects of pastoral and biblical theology, always requiring a practical assignment, which the students were to "re-teach" to others. In most cases, the lessons took the form of small booklets, which could be carried in the students' pockets. "We evangelicals tend to prepare people who can state the doctrine correctly, rather than those who can share the evangel."[39] Patterson's approach proved to prepare people to share the evangel.

Typical TEEE training booklets – 1981.

The example shows one page of text from "La Etica Pastoral," which includes, as always, culturally-appropriate graphics.

In the teaching and direction of the extension meetings, Patterson began to use several key national men as regional leaders so that within three years, by 1972, he saw that it was best to move to La Ceiba. In La Ceiba he was able to set up an extension program office and focus on increased production of lesson

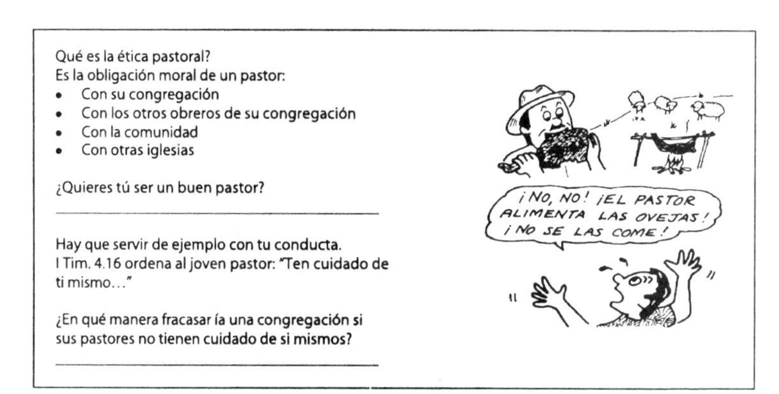

Qué es la ética pastoral?
Es la obligación moral de un pastor:

- Con su congregación
- Con los otros obreros de su congregación
- Con la comunidad
- Con otras iglesias

¿Quieres tú ser un buen pastor?

____

Hay que servir de ejemplo con tu conducta.
I Tim. 4.16 ordena al joven pastor: "Ten cuidado de ti mismo..."

¿En qué manera fracasar ía una congregación si sus pastores no tienen cuidado de si mismos?

____

Example page from "La Etica Pastoral."

materials. This distance from the work also gave the local leaders in Olanchito room to grow and space to blossom as leaders.[40] Also during this time, the extension ministry became a bit more formalized in organizational structure and the name Honduran Extension Bible Institute (HEBI) was chosen for the school.

A Daughter's Testimony – by Anne Patterson Thiessen[41]

Thirty years ago, when my dad, George Patterson, first went to Honduras, the country was ripe for spiritual harvest, especially in the rural areas. Although people considered themselves to be Catholic, the Catholic church did not have the resources to put priests in the villages, and most villagers rarely saw a priest more than once or twice a year. They had neither the animist beliefs of the Indian population nor the daily Mass and Communion of the Catholic Church to channel their spiritual hunger, so when they heard the gospel presented plainly and honestly, they responded by the thousands.

My father's first responsibility upon arriving in Honduras was to teach in the Honduran Bible Institute at Olanchito. He was also expected to pastor the Olanchito church, though he never did. Encouraged by the senior missionary, Jim Clark, he began to see that the trickle of young men graduating from the Bible school were not the natural leaders in their communities. The natural leaders were semi-literate heads of households. He told me how he observed such men looking into the church windows in Olanchito at the congregation of mostly women, but never wanting to come inside. He wondered what it would take to build a church with strong, non-imported leadership.

Nor were the young graduates moving into the surrounding villages to plant churches. Instead, they were moving out to the city churches[42] that offered salaries and status. Meanwhile, the villages continued to starve for the gospel. Somehow the gospel needed to be taken right to the households of these communities.

So, taking members of the Olanchito church with him, my father began to visit homes in the nearby villages, concentrating on heads of households. When people responded to the gospel, he baptized them and recognized them as churches – real churches that served the sacraments and ordained leaders. The first man he baptized was killed with a machete in his own home, his faith an excuse for violence. At his funeral, much of his family turned to Christ and a church was born. I remember when my father came back from that village with machete slashes in the seat of his motorcycle. The gospel was resisted, but could not be withstood.

To disciple the new church leaders, my father introduced a more reproducible system of education. He had been turning over and over in his mind the difficulty in getting semi-literates to study Scripture. One day while sitting on a train and looking around, my dad noticed the passengers reading the photo-novels and comics so popular throughout the Third World. The light came on. He started extension classes right in the leaders' homes, using comic-sized and comic-illustrated study booklets that student-elders could immediately apply and disseminate to their own disciples. Occasionally, the leaders added to the curriculum by writing their own booklets. With the residential Bible Institute shutting down, the Extension Bible Institute (HEBI) became a reproducible tool in new leaders' hands.

Some of the original Bible school graduates felt threatened, even cheated. They felt the new pastors were taking short cuts and weren't properly trained to baptize, serve the Lord's supper, or ordain elders in new churches. They tried to force the new student-elders out of leadership and at one time threatened to get my father expelled from the country. But the churches multiplying under the repro-

ducible style of training quickly outnumbered the traditional churches, and the movement could not be stopped.

Three marks distinguished the movement. ***The first mark*** *was an emphasis on grace. The churches knew the difference between the essentials of the gospel of grace and the human traditions we introduce ourselves. Repentance, faith, baptism, prayer, fellowship around the Lord's Supper, giving and love toward God and others – these are the essentials. Training programs and worship style and requirements for serving or receiving the sacraments reflect human traditions. The Honduran movement experienced a refreshing freedom from the rampant legalism in Latin America, because they knew where their loyalties lay: with grace. On a personal note, the last time we visited the Honduran movement, we asked Humberto Del Arca, the director of the Instituto Bíblico de Extensión (HEBI), about their new work with the Garífuna people. I was especially curious to know what a Latin evangelist would do about the Garífuna penchant for dancing, taboo among Latin evangelicals. His answer amazed me. "We don't prohibit anything!" He wasn't talking about a moral free-for-all; he was talking about grace.*

The second distinguishing mark *of the Honduran movement was relationships of trust. The churches were joined by a network of traveling disciplers who maintained relationships with leaders and their churches. My father told me how once he was running from village to village trying to deal with divisive problems. One of his regional directors pulled him aside and told him to slow down and trust God more. "You're just dancing with the devil," he told him. Because of their strong relationship, this Honduran man felt free to question my father's decisions and help him keep perspective. The style of leadership I saw modeled was never authoritarian. The disciplers served their disciples and gave way to them, passing on authority willingly and joyfully. In 1985, my father left the*

Honduran movement in the hands of the Honduran leaders, giving way for the Spirit to develop their own gifts of leadership. This was the ultimate test of trust, and the Honduran church has grown because of it.

***The third mark** of the Honduran churches on the north coast was obedience to Christ. They distinguished themselves not only by what they believed, but also by what they did. Their goal, a list of seven commands of Christ,[43] was made up of action verbs.*

One of the darkest moments in my father's ministry was when he realized that he had fallen into an old tradition himself. He realized that he had been denying baptism to repentant sinners because they had no legal papers for their marriages. He realized that baptism was being treated as a graduation ceremony for the perfected rather than an entrance ceremony for repentant sinners into the Kingdom. Leaders were essentially telling people not to obey God until they had written permission from the Honduran government. To break with this tradition of requiring legal marriage papers for baptism caused conflict, but through that conflict, the Honduran churches learned the authority of Scripture for themselves, and they learned that obedience to Christ's commands in Scripture comes first, even when tradition points the other way. With so many Western traditions competing for loyalty in Latin America, this beacon helped to keep the church from becoming enslaved by Western culture. Latin America must be obedient to the Lord, not subservient to us and our traditions.

I was privileged to grow up in a great movement of people turning to God all around me on the north coast of Honduras. I was privileged to know great Honduran Christian servant-leaders. I was privileged to watch a people freed to plant church after church within their own culture and beyond. I was privileged to see the Spirit poured out among the Conservative Baptist churches of northern

Honduras, and this vision will always help shape my hope of what the church can be.

In the West, the church has seen phenomenal growth in the past and may yet see it again. But it's obviously in the non-western world that the Spirit's time has come to multiply the church in a way we don't experience in our own home churches in the States. This may be humbling and maybe even threatening to us. We can hinder the Spirit's work if we try to manage it or control it. But there is another way. We can instead look to these new young churches, fresh with the zeal and fire of the Spirit's outpouring, for hope and renewed faith. We can glean from them the vision and encouragement we need to follow Christ in these last days. We can acknowledge ourselves as the elder (and weaker) brother, and enter, with joy, the Father's celebration of his young Prodigal's return home. This was my experience in Honduras.

George Patterson – Pioneer with TEEE[44]

Patterson did not stick with traditional ways as he went about making disciples. For this, he took a lot of flack throughout the '70s and '80s. He was non-traditional. Yet, thousands have been mobilized for service by this servant. He has taken the time to disciple others, coaching them to do the same. That, by far, has been the thread that ties together the many years of this faithful one – discipling others, whether they be poor, rural *campesinos* or young, wet-behind-the-ears *gringos* wanting to learn from a master.

Through the years, Patterson has made disciples who have gone on to many parts of the world. The author of this text heard of Patterson while living in Denver years ago. I was chatting with a seminary friend. My friend heard that I was moving to Los Angeles – the same area where George and Denny lived at the time. My friend Bill exhorted me, "Patrick, when you get to L.A., look up George Patterson. He discipled me years ago. He taught me how to be a missionary. And now I will soon leave for Europe as a missionary."

Years later after George discipled me and trained me to be a missionary, I found myself in the famous La Ceiba central park where I ran into a missionary named Rick Polson, who ministered in Costa Rica. Over lunch that day I asked him his story. His words echoed my friend from Denver with something like this: "Years ago I met George Patterson who trained me how to serve cross-culturally. Now I am a career missionary in Costa Rica."

And the story continues…. In San Pedro Sula, Honduras, I met Rob Thiessen – Patterson's son-in-law and a career missionary to Mexico. His testimony was along these lines: "To this day, George teaches and counsels me."

In Portland, I met Jon Lewis, a 20-year veteran missionary to Argentina who had this to say: "Twenty-three years ago when I was young and with long hair, George took me under his wing, coached me along and got me started in a career of cross-cultural service." Jon went on to become an important missiologist with the World Evangelical Fellowship.

Do we see a theme here? One man discipled others, reproducing his own life and the life of our missionary-hearted Savior into the lives of others. Discipleship took place and lives all over the world have been steered in God's direction.

During the summer 2000 CB meetings in Denver, Colorado, George Patterson was awarded a certificate of appreciation by MTA for his role in faithfully discipling others.

An Association of CB Churches

Beginning in January of 1973, an annual conference was held for three or four days in La Ceiba in order to develop a sense of unity for all the Honduran CB churches. Generally, the conferences included Bible studies and inspirational messages as well as reports from the various churches, the radio station and the HEBI program. Gradually, the plan for an association of Conservative Baptist churches developed. In 1975 at the annual conference in San Pedro Sula, the representatives of various CB churches accepted the first part of a constitution to establish an association, and during the following year the rest of the statutes were drawn up. The annual conference in January of 1976 in La Ceiba ratified these statutes. Later that year the CB association of churches held a constituent assembly in San Pedro Sula to form the "Asociación Cultural Radiofónica," the new national board of HRVC. For some time, the members of the Radio Association board were elected during the annual meetings of the CB association of churches. Years later in the late 1980s, this approach toward a national organization fell apart. From the 1980s on into the new millennium, the various CB regional ministries would continue to maintain unity in terms of relational and spiritual fellowship, but would insist upon a separation relating to organizational and/or hierarchical dynamics. This was due to the socio-economic differences within the various areas of ministry coupled with strong missionary (Honduran and North American) personalities present at the time.

Hurricane Fifi

Hurricane Fifi devastated the north coast of Honduras in September 1974, forcing several missionaries and workers into special tasks. George Patterson found it necessary to work with the relief program in Olanchito and the Aguan Valley. He was named coordinator for that area by the Honduran government and would have collapsed under the strain of the work had it not been for two men who arrived from Oregon right at that precise time. Dick Miller, a civil engineer, came to help build small houses for villagers who lost their dwellings in the flooding of the Aguan River. Jon Lewis, an Argentine missionary's son referred to previously, relieved George in the distribution of the relief supplies. Both men later returned to help with aspects of the extension program.

The relief and rehabilitation efforts, after Fifi, received excellent funds from concerned people in the States. This interest after the hurricane served as a catalyst to additional efforts for social and material betterment on a long-range basis. Patterson and others in La Ceiba created the Asociación de Mutua Ayuda (AMA for short), a cooperative program to help grain farmers get good markets for their products. Eventually, the social and material betterment programs began to be carried on by the north coast churches through the channels of the extension program. Nationwide, several evangelical denominations and missions cooperated in developing the Committee for Evangelical Emergency Aid (Comité Evangélico de Emergéncia Nacional or "CEDEN," in Spanish). Omar Reyes[45] became one of the first presidents of CEDEN. A national director was employed and eventually a full office staff existed with regional offices. A large part of the money to support CEDEN came from the Church World Service. The CB association of churches questioned whether or not it should cooperate with a group that had its income from this World Council of Churches-related organization. However, the association voted to continue cooperation since the doctrinal statement of CEDEN was thoroughly evangelical.

CBs in San Pedro Sula

In 1974, Jim Clark had gotten in touch with two men who started a congregation in Barrio Las Palmas in San Pedro Sula. René Madrid and Miguel Aguilar had founded this church. They had both gone to the Central American Mission Bible Institute in Guatemala City and now sought affiliation with the CBs. In July of 1974, Miguel Aguilar, pastor of the new Las Palmas church, had become the first CBHMS Field Minister partially supported by the Mission's Urban Field Fund. This fund provided limited, descending-scale funds for CB church planting pastors. While the relationship with Aguilar, according to Jim Clark, was rocky at times, Aguilar's leadership as a church pastor paved the way for the CB ministry in San Pedro Sula for years to come. Later, in 1975, René was invited by the

Satélite CB church in Tegucigalpa to serve as pastor. In doing so, Madrid came under the CBHMS descending-scale plan when he became pastor of the Satélite congregation in Tegucigalpa.

Food for Thought – Why or why not are pastoral subsidies by foreign entities a good option? [46]

To Support or Not to Support?

Church-planting missionaries who favor pastoral subsidies from foreign sources point out that support from a "rich brother" fans the flame for men who want to serve. Workers are needed for the harvest and funds permit this. Studies show that pastoral salaries are a means to expedite the church-planting process.

On the opposite side of the scale, church-planting missionaries also argue that foreign support fans economic dependencies. Dependencies create a need for more and more help, resulting in a downward spiral, leading to psychological and social dysfunction such that the church or pastor being "helped" is crippled in their ability to care for their own affairs.[47] Salaried pastors tend to hold their allegiance to the missionary or to the foreign mission agency rather than to the local church. They also tend to view their jobs as just that – a job, rather than a call from God. Wayne Allen, professor of missions in Jamaica, in his research on pastoral subsidies concluded, "The use of subsidies... did not further the cause of Christ. In the districts where it was used, church growth ceased. In the districts where it was not used, growth continued. Clearly, there is something wrong with providing money for national pastors."[48]

The Roman Catholic Church made this error during the Spanish conquest of Central America. During the 300 years of conquest and control, the Roman Catholic Church did not seek to raise up indigenous priests from within Latin America.[49] "The

Spanish and Portuguese American churches were... parasitic. Like the civil governments, they were paternalistically controlled and directed from the mother countries."[50]

Allen provides these guidelines for subsidy use in those cases where it does take place: 1) It should be limited to nationals who are missionaries and evangelists; 2) Indigenous churches should assume responsibility for pastoral support as soon as possible; 3) The indigenous missionaries who start churches are to follow the model of turning over the church to the locals so as to support their own pastor.[51]

As Jesus constantly prepared his disciples for His departure, the prudent missionary anticipates his or her future departure from the field and prepares nationals to function without foreign assistance.

New Church Buildings in Tegucigalpa and San Pedro Sula

During furlough in 1976, Jim Clark sought and found help from the U.S. to get church buildings erected at the Tegucigalpa Satélite church and the San Pedro Sula Las Palmas church. In January and February of 1977, crews of men from Long Prairie, Minnesota and Pennsylvania came to help Satélite build its church. Meanwhile, in San Pedro Sula, the Las Palmas church obtained both a loan from a CBHMS revolving fund toward a building program as well as substantial gifts from a number of friends and churches in the U.S., with their church building dedication in May of that same year.

The Davises Move to La Ceiba

In 1977, after five years of ministry with the Roatan Baptist Academy, Darryl and Nadine Davis moved to La Ceiba as part of the extension program team. Patterson had desperately needed an assistant! Darryl wasted no time

Darryl Davis teaching a lesson – 1981.

in assisting Patterson with HEBI administrative details in La Ceiba. He was also charged with the care of the three churches that had been birthed to the west of Tela. It was during this time that the HEBI-related churches saw the entry of Humberto Del Arca as a teacher.

Humberto Del Arca explains how the chain-reaction training principle has resulted in many churches being started throughout northern Honduras – 1985.

It was during these years that the HEBI-related churches began to identify themselves as a regional association area, which was uniquely related to the HEBI training program. This was partly due to the socio-economic differences between the HEBI-related churches and those of the other Honduran sectors (e.g., Tegucigalpa and San Pedro Sula), but also due to the differences in philosophy of ministry that existed between the rural and the city churches. Ultimately, during the late 1980s, such separateness was due to a need for self-preservation, amidst city folks who wanted to radically cease the extension ministry approach among the north coast ministries.[52] In all this, the church association of the north coast area was tied as one organizational unit with the school.[53] This would remain so and set the flavor for ministry for decades to come.

The Clarks Move to El Salvador

As early as the '60s, pastors in El Salvador began listening to HRVC and inquired about the Conservative Baptist work. CBHMS missionaries from Honduras visited El Salvador in 1971 at the invitation of the Baptist churches there, but no CB ministry for El Salvador was set up at that time. When in 1977 the Salvadorean men renewed contact, Jim Clark visited San Salvador to look into the development of a ministry. Impressed by the vast poverty-stricken housing areas and other factors in San Salvador, the Clarks decided to move there to begin a new work. In October of 1977, their move was completed. They would minister there until May of 1979, just in time for the civil wars which would ignite the country during the 1980s. They left the Mission around this time.

Years after Jim Clark had left Honduras, this writer was in the poor beach-side community of El Porvenir on the north coast. I was "spying out" the land for new church plant areas and also getting to know a local man – Eusebio. Talking with him, he told me of how he came to the Lord years earlier. "An American missionary made weekly visits to the government hospital in Tegucigalpa, where I was sick. He led me to the Lord and followed-up with me each week. I have been walking with the Lord since." I asked him, "What was the missionary's name?" He said, "Jaime Clark" and quickly produced from his weather-worn wooden cabinet an old and tattered prayer card from the '70s of Jim and Hazel Clark. They looked so young! I was floored and I rejoiced in the Lord for this testimony about a fellow missionary.

As chance would have it, I lost contact with Eusebio, but several years later, coincidentally enough, I met another man in a different town with the same last name. The new man I met turned out to be Eusebio's younger brother, Victor. Following Jim's impact in Eusebio's life, that testimony was passed on to Victor through the family. Ultimately in the 1990s, Victor Almendarez would come to the Lord, be discipled by this writer and even come on with the Mission as a national missionary, as we shall read more of later. We see the circle of life here, the trail of connectedness in Christ: from the Mission (through Jim) to Eusebio to Victor and back to the Mission. Jim's effect is still felt to this day through folks like Eusebio, Victor and others.

The Period of Nationalized Leadership Structures – 1985 to 2000

The HEBI Ministry Nationalized

By the mid 1980s, the HEBI ministry had birthed nearly 150 churches. Nearly all of the churches were started by the extension students on the north coast, and not by the missionaries. This is a positive testimony to the ability with which the missionaries mobilized the nationals.

The philosophy of ministry was (and still is) pretty much summarized in a call for local church ministries to be localized at all costs – localized leadership, localized funding, etc. Foreign elements generally weaken indigenous churches. Wise missionaries, though present and active in their respective areas, will work cautiously to prevent themselves from being stumbling blocks to localized infrastructures. Sadly, many missionaries, oblivious to these simple principles which the Lord used to birth our CB movement on the north coast, blindly interact on the field so as to unwittingly create maximum dependency and cripple indigenity.[54]

Interestingly, for his work on the north coast and for the way in which he mobilized nationals for maximum indigenity, George Patterson was awarded an honorary Doctor of Divinity from his alma mater, Western Seminary, Portland, Oregon. He comments, "People tell me that I started all these churches. What I did was to mobilize others to start new works." This is the golden secret that so many of us never catch on to. Like Paul the Apostle, Patterson simply discipled men who were coached in discipling others. As they obeyed this command, the Lord blessed the work. Through HEBI, a national movement of CB churches was birthed, which to this day tends to be the prized pearl of the CB work in Central America.

Food for Thought – Will we, as a Mission, seek out new "pearls"? What new areas of ministry await us? The Moskito Coast? Cuba? The West Indies?[55]

On the north coast, the organization of students and pastoral activities was maintained through regional, geographical areas led by HEBI "regional directors." Each regional director – himself an extension student – was accountable to the HEBI director. For many years, George Patterson served the area as HEBI's director. After a two-year transition beginning in 1983, the HEBI leadership was turned over to Honduran men. Humberto Del Arca was appointed to lead HEBI. He, with his board of regional directors, made up the HEBI executive board and the church association leadership team.

It was at this time, in 1985, that Del Arca was also invited to become a CBHMS Senior Field Minister. Through the years, Humberto Del Arca would show himself to be a calm-spirited man of God. Humberto is the forever cool, self-contained man who regards argument as dissonant noise that would only disrupt the natural harmonies of his own life. He, with his wife Carmen, set the pace for the growing movement of CB churches in north-central Honduras.

George Patterson (left) and Darryl Davis (right) turn over the leadership of the Honduras Extension Bible Institute to Humberto Del Arca – 1985.

This relationship with the Mission proved positive for the Mission and for the Honduran churches in that it permitted an ongoing relationship between the two through the decades. Though he moved back to the States,[56] Patterson would continue as an outside counselor of sorts, preparing studies for "Humberto and the gang" for many years. Humberto was one of the Mission's pride and joy's on into the new millennium. And rightly so, as he led the north coast ministry with a steady hand and an immovable mooring of character and intimacy with God. While a godly man, Humberto was far from being an administrator. Thus, through the years of his tenure, he was vitally assisted by three secretaries: Betty Gale, who later perished in an auto accident in La Ceiba in 2000; Yolanda Matute and Milanova Reyes. Yet, while the HEBI ministry was effectively nationalized, it remains none-the-less dependent on foreign funds.

Roatan Island Ministry During the 1980s and 1990s

As we have seen previously, CB missionaries have had an ongoing witness on Roatan Island for many years. The Davises served on Roatan from 1973 to 1978, the Millers for eight years during the 1980s and Ruth Palnick for a time toward the end of the 1990s.

In 1984, CBHMS missionaries John and Hope Miller were invited by Glen Solomon to come to Roatan to aid in church development and pastoral training. Several students were preparing for ministry and the local pastors were making good progress, yet additional leadership training by the Millers was needed. During John Miller's last year on the island, he was attacked and stabbed. And his life was threatened. For this rea-

Glen Solomon directed the ministry of eight churches on Roatan and also served as Governor of Roatan – 1981.

son, with other factors in place as well, he elected to return to the States to serve the Mission in other ways.

Roatan saw the presence of MTA[57] missionary Ruth Palnick during the late 1990s. Ruth spent a year and a half there on loan to World Gospel Mission, running a clinic in the community of Punta Gorda. While on the island, Ruth was able to minister with the Baptist churches begun by previous CBHMS missionaries. A few more details regarding her time on the island and with the Mission in Tegucigalpa are described later in this section.

Baby Churches in San Pedro Sula

In 1986, the Las Palmas church planted a daughter church in the La Central sector of Barrio Rivera Hernandez. This daughter church soon planted two additional CB churches – in Rivera Hernandez and in La Montanita.

Throughout the late '80s, the four San Pedro Sula churches showed minimal to nominal growth. In the mid '90s, three of the four San Pedro Sula churches brought on new pastors and each new pastor was used by God to vitally enhance the inner stability of their respective churches.

Quinteen Linares served as pastor to the Las Palmas church throughout the '90s and into the first years of 2000. His church grew to such a degree that, largely with their own resources, they enlarged their worship sanctuary. The Las Palmas church began the year 2000 with around 16 vibrant cell groups.

Luis Rodulfo Padilla served as pastor to the La Central church through the 1990s and into the first years of 2000. Under his iron-fisted leadership, his church began the year 2000 with around six functioning cell groups.

This church built a pastoral house for Pastor Luis with their own funds. While the pastor had no formal Bible training, he proved himself a good leader who was grounded in the Word through personal studies. His church was instrumental in preparing Victor Almendarez during Victor's first few years as a believer. Pastor Luis had previously worked with the CB churches in the Agua Dulce, Atlantida area on the north coast.

Arnold Linares (no relation to Quinteen Linares) served throughout the '90s and into the first years of 2000 as pastor to the Rivera Hernandez church. Arnold had come to Christ through MTA's N.T. Dellinger and quickly began to prepare himself for ministry. Pastor Linares received formal pastoral training through the San Pedro Sula Southern Baptist Seminary where he graduated from a three-year course of studies and where he met his wife. He also finished a few classes with HEBI-West. Under his gentle, godly leadership, his church saw six functioning cell groups at the turn of the century. While the worship services have never really been "packed" like the Las Palmas church and the La Central church, the church has had a stable membership of around 50 with grounded lay leaders in place. Various leaders within this church studied with HEBI-West and discipleship has been a key emphasis within this church. New converts are carefully followed up with little apparent attrition. Arnold's church has internal stability and strength as an organism and organization. The Rivera Hernandez church built a new and extremely large church building during Arnold's pastorate with close to no foreign support. It is interesting to note that the above three churches grew in many ways, yet with minimal foreign monetary assistance. Is there a correlation between inner church strength and non-dependency on foreign funds? While the above three churches have been quite strong, the La Montanita church has never been so. It experienced a church split in 1998.

MTA Missionary Activities in San Pedro Sula During the 1990s

MTA Belize-based missionary N.T. Dellinger visited the San Pedro Sula churches during the mid-1990s. He has brought friendship, counsel, direction and occasional teaching times to the churches. Patrick O'Connor began visiting the San

Pedro churches every week in late 1994. His involvement was primarily through discipleship-oriented relationships and through one-on-one extension pastoral training studies from 1994 through to the late 1990s. Patrick's wife Debbie worked with the women, the youth leaders and the Sunday school teachers during this time, having weekend conferences for the leaders now and again. Patrick and Debbie lived in San Pedro Sula in 1996, during which time they focused their ministry on the four churches. They attempted to enhance existing church infrastructures without creating dependencies. Sensing that this was accomplished, the O'Connors felt at liberty to move on to the western mountains. Overall, then, the San Pedro Sula CB churches have been autonomous and indigenous with each pursuing its respective destiny.

Patrick and Debbie O'Connor, Katie, Sarah – 2000.

The overall context for ministry in San Pedro Sula in which the four CB churches exist includes these factors:

- There are more than 400 evangelical churches accounted for in San Pedro Sula. This figure does not include new unrecorded churches being planted monthly.
- Evangelical churches as a whole are doing well with aggressive outreach as a visible, tangible indicator of strength. One example of this church life is the Southern Baptists who have a San Pedro Sula Association made up of 19 organized churches and 17 church plants.[58] Another church (La Iglesia Quadrangular) recorded a membership of more than 20,000 members with more than 1000 cell groups.[59]
- Local missionaries have commented on the sense of loving, friendly competition by various evangelical churches to start church plants in communities. The sense is, "If we

do not plant a church in such-and-such a community, then another evangelical church will. Let's get to work!"

With these factors in place, two valid approaches to ministry in San Pedro Sula are possible:[60]

1. A "Let's-win-this-city" approach. This approach keeps in mind that many opportunities for growth and outreach within the CB work are still at hand. A qualified CB missionary operating within the correct cultural and ministerial parameters (i.e., a desire to raise up local leaders) could have a viable ministry with: a) CB church plants and/or b) an emphasis on youth among the existing CB churches.
2. A "Let's-go-to-a-needier-area" approach. This approach would not focus on San Pedro Sula, reasoning that the Kingdom of God is pretty much functioning well there. This approach would address a desire to minister in needier areas in Honduras or Central America.

Hector and Sylvia Newman in Tegucigalpa

The Newmans were appointed by the Mission in June of 1978 and arrived in Honduras in March of 1980. Hector had previously served in various churches in the Boston area before sensing a call to return to his native homeland of Honduras with their two children, Hector Enrique and Maritza. While the Newmans were reared in the States, both were born in Central America.

In appointing the Newmans, the Mission asked Hector to focus his energies on church planting in Tegucigalpa and the surrounding areas. And that they did! Hector used the pastoral approach[61] to start churches to the end that within a span of ten years, the Lord used him to plant eight new CB churches, bringing the number of CB churches in Tegucigalpa from two to ten during the decade. Like other missionaries dedicated to faithful service, the Newmans changed the spiritual face of a needy city. This is a listing of the CB churches in Tegucigalpa as of 1990:

✓ Iglesia Bautista Conservadora de Colonia Satélite

✓ Iglesia B.C. de Miraflores

✓ Iglesia B.C. de Colonia San José de la Pena*

✓ Iglesia B.C. de Colonia Las Torres*

✓ Iglesia B.C. de Colonia Los Robles*

✓ Iglesia B.C. de Colonia Germánia*

✓ Iglesia B.C. de Colonia Santa Rosa*

✓ Iglesia B.C. de Colonia Altos de Loarque*

✓ Iglesia B.C. de Colonia Villeda Morales*

✓ Iglesia B.C. de Colonia Las America*

* Churches which Hector Newman played a vital role in starting.

With eight new and growing CB churches, the Newmans sensed a need for a training school to provide leadership preparation. It was at this time that Hector founded the Conservative Baptist Bible School.

Not wanting to slow down, Hector took the time to also found other ministries:

➢ Centro Cristiano de Orientacion Psicologica which is a counseling ministry specifically geared toward meeting family-related needs for families in crisis. The ministry seeks to instruct, counsel and encourage people within a biblical worldview.

➢ The National Association of Christian Ministries which has united ministries of various denominations and has organized quite a few national evangelistic crusades.

➢ The CB National Christian Camp which, as of this writing, is being started on 14 acres of forest land in the mountains east of Tegucigalpa.

While working interdenominationally with the above new ministries, Hector showed no desire to slow down efforts to start new CB works. He branched out beyond the Tegucigalpa area to partner with other nationals in forming new CB churches in other departments, forming quite a few additional churches during the 1990s in these areas:

- ✓ Dulce Nombre de Copán
- ✓ Comayagua
- ✓ La Paz
- ✓ La Esperanza
- ✓ Danlí
- ✓ Villa Santa of El Paraiso
- ✓ Valle Bonito of Comayagua
- ✓ Colonia Villa Bertilia in the city of Choluteca

In spite of the many ways in which the Lord used Hector and Sylvia as MTA missionaries, they resigned from the Mission in early 2001 for personal reasons.

Ruth Palnick in Tegucigalpa[62]

Ruth Palnick was appointed with the Mission in July 1989. After a year in Costa Rica studying Spanish, Ruth arrived in Honduras on January 25, 1991, which is Honduras' "Day of the Woman."

After a year of acculturation during which time she did a bit of teaching in the Conservative Baptist Bible School, Ruth began implementing TEE principles to equip pastors and leaders in the metropolitan area of Tegucigalpa. She used the ever-popular SEAN materials of Chile, South America. These materials had been used for years in the CB URBACAD (Urban Academy Leadership Education) courses in the States. Ruth's TEE ministry in Tegucigalpa followed the purposes and plans established by CB missionaries on the north coast of Honduras, which was to provide preparation for pastors and leaders within existing church ministries.

Over the next four years, Ruth began various URBACAD programs. The intent was always that Ruth would only teach the first three-year cycle and then one of the graduates would continue. The courses were established in five churches and completed in four. In three of the four churches, on-going classes continue to this day, led by former graduates. Overseeing all of the work is Delmer Degado, pastor of the Germánia CB Baptist Church. It is notable that within five years, over half of the Germánia congregation had graduated from URBACAD.

Women learn how to teach and share their faith during the Gracias, Lempira national women's conference – 2001.

Ruth's evangelism and focus on discipleship and training of leaders brought great joy to her heart in seeing the spiritual growth evident in lives that God had transformed. In the 1998 national conference for women hosted in Tegucigalpa by the leaders in the Germánia church, for example, there were young women who taught entire seminars. This is significant in that a few short years earlier they had been too shy to even look up in class, let alone stand to teach entire seminars. As they imparted God's truth to their fellow countrywomen, many were amazed in seeing how far they had come as a result of Ruth's ministry.

Since this work had so effectively been taken over by Honduran leaders, Ruth was able to return to her field of nursing. The following years found her becoming very involved in a Honduras-based clinic, which ministered to inner-city people with HIV and AIDS. Located in the heart of Tegucigalpa's "red light" district, Ruth was nurse and chaplain in an evangelistic and discipleship ministry to a truly hidden and very needy people group. For three years, Ruth saw God work in amazing ways as many of these patients and family members came to Jesus Christ. A number of Honduran believers joined in this work and, during Ruth's ministry with the clinic, several Honduran teams visited. Funds were given by Hondurans, which left the clinic in better shape, and with more resources with which to continue the work. During this time, Ruth was also placed on loan to a clinic in Punta Gorda, Roatan, during which time Hurricane Mitch came for a visit.

Due to some severe health problems, Ruth was forced to return to the States at the end of 1998. She remained with MTA, serving as a hospital and hospice chaplain in the Phoenix, Arizona, area.

Western Honduras Extension Bible Institute – HEBI-West, 1996 to Present

While Patrick and Debbie O'Connor were in La Ceiba, the Mission asked them to learn the HEBI model and the church planting by extension model with the hope that it could be replicated in a new area. For this reason, when the O'Connors moved to Santa Rosa de Copán, a main intention was to not simply set in motion chains of new churches, but also to establish a daughter institute to HEBI. Thus, HEBI-West was started. It followed the model of the mother school, but also "tweaked" the study program a bit. One area of adjustment was to keep the organizational leadership structure of HEBI-West as a separate entity from the new CB churches in western Honduras. Patrick saw HEBI-West as a para-church ministry that would work alongside the churches, not controlling them in any way. Another area of change was the vision to permit non-CB pastors the chance to study with HEBI-West. The need for such training is desperate. The Lord honored this openness to teach and train non-CBs with the result that more than 400 students were studying by extension as of 1999. In 2001, the Mission appointed a national –

Typical Western Honduras town.

Ambrosio Cordoba – to work with HEBI-West in Copán. Ambrosio and his wife, Norma, were gifted saints and had been involved with the north coast CB churches in Trujillo, Colón and Yoro, Yoro for years. He would later assume the HEBI-West directorship, freeing the O'Connors to move on to a new area and to happily experience the dream of a ministry started and successfully turned over to national hands.

Spontaneous Multiplication in Western Honduras – 1997 to Present

Spontaneous multiplication of churches relates to an ideal missionary situation in which trained nationals – having been trusted with the reigns of leadership – reproduce themselves and their own new indigenous churches in a way that is rapid, efficient and inexpensive. Observers said it was mind-boggling to see the Spirit of God birthing such indigenous churches through spontaneous multiplication in the western mountains.

The Mission witnessed the Spirit moving in the mountains of western Honduras through Victor Almendarez and his amazing team of men. While the Lord used Patrick O'Connor to pioneer and begin the movement through the birthing of the first cluster of CB churches in Copán, He brought Victor into place at the right time to advance the movement into Lempira. Victor raised up men, who with limited means, met regularly for all-night prayer meetings and who, with efficient use of energy, traveled through the mountains entering new rural towns to make more disciples. "New churches in rural towns

Victor Almendarez (far left) and Patrick O'Connor (second from right) with three national CB pastors in Copán – 1996.

where there is no evangelical church" was their vision and battle cry.

This writer has many recollections of how these churches grew. One was a simple baptism, typical of many during the late 1990s. The La Florida church met with the San Nicolás church for baptisms in the river. Fifty came to watch as three mature men and three women obeyed the Lord publicly. Three truckloads of people made their way down the rocky paths to the river to introduce tears and softly sung hymns about the Lord's forgiveness to the baptism event. Such baptisms seemed to take place monthly.

In Zarzal de Lempira, a six-month-old CB church had their temple dedication in 1998. The church was started by one of Victor's disciples. It was in a town in the backwoods (no electricity, etc.) up from Gracias one hour on a very bad "road." With the exception of a $90 gift from Canada, this new church covered all it's own costs – donated land, donated building and repairs to the building.

In an electricity-less remote place called Camalote, a church building dedication was held in which more than 400 people came. The dedication was followed by their own three-day missions conference. The Camalote CB church was eight months old in the Lord and had already mothered two daughter churches. The Mission rejoiced to hear of new chains of churches in rural, isolated places. This had been the O'Connors' vision.

This writer also recalls leaving early from an all-night vigil in celebration of a new church building built by the nationals in the rural outback. He stumbled through the forest with a makeshift torch above his head and a weak-batteried flashlight in his nervous hand. What gripped him as he panted and made his way down the narrow, muddy and rocky path was that he kept passing crowds of people walking up the hill in the darkness to the vigil. More than 200 sleepy-eyed faithful stayed up that night to worship the living God in their mud-walled church and to thank

Him for the new structure. Victor – the military-styled, disciplined, though loving, leader – had his bi-monthly leaders meeting the next morning from 4 to 6 a.m., which was his custom.

Overall, many occasions are recalled in which there was a profound sense of the hand of the living God at work in their midst creating a spontaneous multiplication within an indigenous context.

Western Honduras – A Testimonial by MTA Field Minister Victor Almendarez[63]

Years ago in 1995, I felt the call to be a part of the Lord's big work. It was then that I met Patrick O'Connor. The Lord placed him in my path to become my spiritual teacher.

You see, I was working in a factory in San Pedro Sula back then when the Lord started using me. First, though I was still a new believer, He helped me to organize a Bible study group with the Christians at work and then He helped me to evangelize my co-workers during the bus ride back and forth to work. Deep in my heart, however, I wanted to do something bigger for the Lord. So I began praying for a full-time opportunity in His ministry.

In 1996 He answered my prayer and gave me the privilege of pastoring a church in the state of Copán. It was a small rural community just a bit on the northwest side of Santa Rosa called Dulce Nombre de Copán. My time here coincided with Patrick and Debbie's arrival from San Pedro Sula to Santa Rosa de Copán in September 1996.

Victor and Virgilia Almendarez – 1998.

While I served as Pastor in Dulce Nombre, the Lord saw fit to use Patrick to begin the CB church planting by extension ministry in this area. The Lord raised up churches quite quickly in three areas: San Nicolás de Copán, La Cumbre de Copán and La Florida de Copán. There was also a work in El Prado de la Cruz (Copán), but it did not last.

Though I loved this ministry as a pastor, I once again felt that there was something else for me to do, so that's when He called me to work as an extension teacher with Patrick for the Western Honduras Extension Bible Institute (HEBI-West). The ministry consisted of training pastors and church leaders, but it also meant that we would attempt to start churches in new areas where there were none, all within the state of Copán. This took place in 1997. An MTA missionary intern, Andrew Wachsmuth, lived with my family during this year. He was so much fun to have with us and we took the time to teach him about our culture and the ministry here. He fit in well. In 1999, Andrew returned with a Canadian wife in tow, living in Copán Ruins as a "tentmaker" of sorts for one year.

Dedication of the La Cumbre de Copán church – Summer, 1999.

In January 1998, I began as sub-director of HEBI-West and the Lord took me to the state of Lempira, where our CB churches and our MTA Mission had not done any work previously. We worked hard during this year to begin new churches following the concept of church planting by extension. I discipled men in various hard-to-get-to rural areas. I trained and coached them to lead new outreaches in their respective towns. By mid-1999, we had seen the Lord start around 15 churches as a result. This number includes the new churches in Copán. Some of the areas in Lempira where we have seen new CB churches are these:

- ✓ *Camalote*
- ✓ *Los Ranchos*
- ✓ *El Pinal San José*
- ✓ *El Pinal San Antonio*
- ✓ *Zarzal*
- ✓ *Cedros de Mejicalpa*
- ✓ *Consolaca*
- ✓ *El Limón*
- ✓ *La Union (three churches here)*
- ✓ *Talgua*

Our church planting philosophy is based on the Apostle Paul's approach as shown in II Timothy 2:2. Each church has its own local pastor (a man from the community, not brought in from outside). Each new church also has a leaders' (or elders') council. We have seen that in most cases the local church provided for its own need of a church building in which to worship. We have also seen at least one or two of the new churches (for example, in Camalote de Lempira) start programs to feed the children of the poor. We are happy that one new church even has a literacy program for adults.

As an association of CB churches, we have organized a pastors council at the state level (for the two states of Lempira and Copán). What

Camalote de Lempira CB church – 2000.

we do is to gather all of the pastors from the two states once every two months. During this time, we take turns giving reports on the church's activities. We also have teaching times and hold an all night vigil. We then have our leaders meeting from 4 a.m. to 6 a.m. We depart for our respective homes at 6 a.m.

In 1999, the Lord provided us with two of the pastors to serve as regional supervisors to assist me with the work being done with the new churches. Additionally, they bring the offerings, which the churches have been giving to the association to support missions. In November, 1999, the association chose to support one of our own men to work as a national missionary in a new, needy area called San Jeronimo de Copán, where almost 100 percent of the population is Catholic. We rejoice that the Lord has already saved nearly 25 persons there through our national missionary, Francisco Méndez and his wife, Catarina.

Cory Keith assisting with the construction of the church in San Jeronimo de Copán – Summer, 2000.

It has not always been easy. It has been hard in some areas, as we have found ourselves threatened now and again by others. But the Lord has been faithful and the doors of Hades have not prevailed against the Church of the Lord. In all of this we have tried to be faithful. We are happy that our pastors continue being trained through the extension program of the Western Honduran Extension Bible Institute.

A Truly Indigenous Work?

One of the hopes that Patrick and Debbie had in their work regarding the birth of the movement of CB churches in western Honduras was to facilitate indigenization, nationalization and non-dependent relationships from the start. Simple steps were taken to do this. The O'Connors tried hard, for example, to always insist on localized leadership structures and localized participatory decision-making. Their prompt departure from the scene in 1999 – which could have been seen by some as premature and unnecessary – was part of that simple plan to lay the work upon the shoulders of the nationals.

Food for Thought – What is indigenization and why is it needed? How is it distinguished from a work that is nationalized? How is it distinguished from a work that is economically dependent on foreign funds?

Two Crucial Concepts

Indigenization relates to the cultural "flavor" of the ministry. A work or church is indigenous when it looks like and feels like the local culture. A church or ministry with imported forms is not indigenous. While indigenization relates to the look and feel of the ministry, nationalization relates to localized leadership structures.

A nationalized work is a ministry or church that has local persons as her leaders. Works may be indigenous, but not nationalized until the day when nationals are her primary leaders. While our Mission has taken great care to respect localized leadership authorities – even those associated with the Mission as national missionaries – some mission agencies muddy the water in this area as they control, to varying degrees, the in-place national workers. Thus, while a work may be nationalized, its degree of nationalization and its ability to grow indigenously is compromised when a mission agency holds too much sway in the lives or the decision processes of the national leaders. A no-strings-attached approach, while risky, often fosters better missiological nationalization. A no-strings-attached approach will also free up mission personnel for new unreached areas as opposed to a maintenance mode by the missionaries for years (decades?) to come. Wise missionaries will limit the introduction of foreign devices to local churches (whether they be manners of dress, manners of speech, or manners of funding), so as to foster nationalized leadership that is not only indigenous, but also non-dependent on any foreign devices.

This having been said, mission agencies must also be cautious not to lunge to the opposite extreme in which, for example, a halt is placed on the entry of all foreign personnel. This took place during the early '70s when some missiologists called for a moratorium on western missionaries to Africa. On our own home front, a CB missionary recently commented in an email to me, "Eventually I would like... the North American missionaries removed entirely," which is nothing less than a drift to such an extreme. There must be balance. Looking to the greater picture and wider perspective of ministry, as MTA has done, mission agencies generally employ balance by aiming for nationalization, yet by using foreign missionaries in supportive, complementary ways. Balance is seen as foreign missionaries serve as support personnel. It is also seen as foreign missionaries open up new fields within already existing countries, such as when CB missionaries opened up San José or even western Honduras. The two crucial concepts of indigenization and nationalization can be in balance with the presence of foreign missionaries.

Nationals as Board-appointed Missionaries

As far back as the early 1950s, CBHMS made a radical decision to appoint nationals as missionaries. This policy is practically unheard of among other North American mission agencies. While not common, a case can be made that it has been both a positive strategic move toward mobilizing men and women within their own countries as well as a preparatory move toward new trends in missions. The 1900s has been the century of the North American missionary movement. The USA had taken this missionary-sending baton from England and Germany[64] and will likely pass the baton on to third-world countries within the next 50 years. Should the decline in moral fabric that is eating away the American culture complement a serious economic downturn in this new century, it is likely that this, with other factors, will create a climate whereby the North American church unwittingly ceases to be the forerunner for sending missionaries abroad. Learning from history, Spain and Portugal were the missionary-sending powerhouses for Catholic missionaries during the 1600s and 1700s – during their reign as world economic superpowers.[65] When they ceased to be strong economically due to the expenditures of many wars, they ceased to send out great numbers of missionaries and thus were forced to pass the missionary-sending baton not only to other Catholic regions, but also to the Protestant regions of northern Europe. As it relates to us in the year 2000, we already see a trend in place for third-world nationals to take the baton. Our Mission has been one step ahead of this trend, permitting third-world nationals full missionary status from as early as 1952.

A New Ministry in Copán Ruins of Western Honduras

Patrick O'Connor during a visit to Carizalon, a Chortí Indian community – 1999.

Patrick and Debbie O'Connor reported being thrilled to fully turn over the Copán and Lempira area to the nationals in 1999 so they could move to the new area of Copán Ruins.

Copán Ruins is a small, rural, isolated mountain village on the far edge of western Honduras, minutes from the Guatemalan border. Patrick sensed a desire to reach out to the Chortí Indians who live up in the hills around Copán Ruins. The O'Connors needed to shift gears quite a bit to an even slower pace of life there in that quaint, rustic mountain town of 7,000. Their prayer has been to enter into the hearts and lives of the Chortí. The Chortí Indians descended from the Mayans and throughout the Copán valley there are thousands of ancient Mayan statues, mini-pyramids and artifacts.

Ancient Mayan statue.

While Debbie finds the Chortí fascinating, her first love has been to mobilize the CB women for ministry. One way by which she has done this has been through having seasonal women's conferences, which she began years before in La Ceiba. She rejoices that national women caught this vision and proceeded to have annual conferences on a national level. Each year, more and more women come, with several hundred in attendance in 1999 at the site of the West End, Roatan Island CB church. During the Gracias, Lempira national women's conference in 2000, the women raised 25,000 Lempiras (the equivalent of nearly $2,000) to go toward national missionaries. Debbie is a true missionary at heart. Ironically, when first converted in 1980, one of the first things she told the Lord was, "Lord, I love you and I will do anything… but please do not make me be a missionary." The Lord proceeded to then lead her as a single missionary to Mitla, Oaxaca (Mexico) and Mexico City for a two-

Attendees at a national women's conference in La Ceiba – 2001.

year stint with Wycliffe Bible Translators. She fell in love with the Latin culture and the missionary lifestyle and now says that she wants nothing less than to serve the Lord cross-culturally!

Working with George Patterson, Patrick computerized and edited what became known as the ***Preparación para Movilizacion***.[66] Using a bit of marketing and business background with a touch of creativity, Patrick re-edited and "manualized" Patterson's text and made it ready for a new market. These manuals became quite popular. Not only did the 250 CB churches in Central America look favorably upon them, but several other mission agencies and Bible Institutes in Honduras adapted them as their primary TEE curriculum. Missionaries throughout Latin America, and also from as far away as Australia, Africa and Europe, got ahold of the pastoral manuals and quickly took advantage of their user-friendly style.

Hurricane Mitch – October, 1998

Under the leadership of MTA missionaries Humberto Del Arca, Jeff Brady, Darryl Davis and with the vital assistance of CB church member Rigoberto Reyes, reconstruction projects were facilitated in response to this devastating hurricane, which took the lives of thousands along the north coast and in the capital city. Within the CB circles alone, 181 houses were destroyed, 207 families lost belongings, 11 churches were destroyed or damaged, the La Ceiba HRVC radio tower was destroyed and the Tegucigalpa area CB camp was damaged. By the grace of God, the tireless hard work of many and the generous funding of supporters throughout the world, many CB churches and church family homes were rebuilt and repaired. 150 homes were also built in La Ceiba – establishing the new community of Barrio Botillo, four kilometers south of the airport. And 50 homes were also built in Sonaqura, Colón.

Update on HRVC

With the assistance of Hector Newman as president of the board, HRVC grew during the '90s in two new ways. HRVC not only began to produce as many as a dozen programs each week, but also raised great quantities of money from within the country to establish a network of repeater stations throughout Honduras to the end that HRVC has become the most popular Christian radio channel. As of this writing, preparations are being made to use satellite technology to make HRVC an international radio station.

Partnership Ministries in Honduras and Other Parts of Central America[67]

Throughout the 1990s and into the new millennium, MTA's Partnership Ministries (PM) has brought great numbers of short-term groups from the U.S. to work hand-in-hand with the churches in Central America and the Caribbean. The Lord said, "By this all men will know you are My disciples, if you have love, one for another" (John 13:35). Convinced that Central Americans (and the world in general) needed to see such love from their wealthy brothers to the north and convinced that U.S. Christians must be tangibly reconciled with their brothers to the south, CB missionary Steve Reed began PM.

Steve's background is fascinating! From it we see how God uniquely prepared this special saint for reconciling others to Himself. In college he had become quite active with the Republican Party. He actively worked on a legislative campaign and a gubernatorial campaign. He was even asked to be a youth director for a U.S. senatorial campaign. Because of his commitment to politics and his lack of commitment to college, his grades dropped and he was forced to enter the Army during the Vietnam crisis. He later realized and became convinced that politics was not the solution to life's great problems. He searched for a more enduring solution. What would it be?

In Vietnam, Steve spent fifteen months in combat gear as an engineer. He spent most of his time stationed in the hot, humid and poverty-stricken central highlands. He encountered first-hand the helpless and tragic suffering of poor, innocent Vietnamese. Being still young, his inner values were adjusted and fine-tuned toward a future that would orient itself toward care for the poor. This time in Vietnam may have also contributed toward Steve's tendency to be a highly combustible, ever combative, occasional mile-a-minute talker whose favorite form of conversation is an argument.

Sandwiched between these two value-adjusting events, Steve came to know Christ. It happened during a time of confusion when a close friend frankly confronted Steve. In July of 1971, Steve found the Man who provided real solutions to life's real problems. Steve's life was forever changed. As with many new converts in their young twenties, God had a lot of work to do in Steve's life.

In 1975 Steve met the gal who would become his best friend and life partner, Laura. Laura had been a full-time staff member with Campus Crusade for Christ.

Following Steve's completion of a Master of Divinity from Denver Seminary and Laura's completion of her MBA in the late '70s, the two spent the next ten years living and ministering in the Central American community within the inner city of San Francisco. Steve started and pastored a CB inner-city, Spanish-speaking church called La Iglesia de Nuestro Salvador, comprised predominately of Central Americans.

It was from this setting that the Lord moved within Steve and Laura's hearts to create Partnership Ministries (PM) under the MTA banner. PM was created to not only assist First- and Third-World Christians with reconciliation one to another, but also proved to be vital in providing a significant help to CB churches in Central America. CB churches in Central America oftentimes met in homes or other less-than-adequate locations to worship God. While these indigenous and dynamic congregations worshiped the Lord in Spirit and in Truth, their heart's desire was to worship in a church building. They loved the Lord, yet yearned to have a special meeting place that was more than a simple shack. Steve observed that these holy, Latin saints did not need help in evangelism. Neither did they require help with planting new churches. These humble, yet beautiful people hoped for the day when they would be helped with needed church buildings. *Presto* – Steve and Laura discovered their new and valuable niche.

Steve's ministries of partnership have been centered on the feeling that Christians must plead the cause of the disenfranchised poor. Early on in his walk with Christ, Steve grasped that true Christian love must be demonstrated through Christ-like sacrifice. He learned that Christians must live out gestures of sacrifice among the disenfranchised poor. Such gestures of sacrifice have resulted in more than 100 Partnership Ministries projects in Central America during the 1990s.

With Steve at the helm, PM has had some gifted folks assist with PM leadership, including Mike and Lisa Ratzky,[68] Becky Janda, Mark and Brenda Hall, Victoria de la Cruz and others.

Food for Thought – What interplay are foreign helps-oriented ministries to have with on-the-field missionaries and nationals who long toward living out the three-self principles – self-funding, self-leadership and self-propagation? How do building projects relate to the three-self principles?

Jeff and Nancy Brady – Serving on the North Coast, 1999 to Present

This writer had the chance to visit Jeff and Nancy Brady in La Ceiba in preparation of this information. It was a time when I needed a "shot in the arm" that sometimes only fellow missionaries can provide. Boy, did I get it! I was encouraged in my faith and awe-struck as I saw what the Lord was doing through them.

What I found was a middle-aged couple who had sold their Washington State-based business to become missionaries. They continue to maintain another business – Brady Trucking of Shelton, WA – so as to serve Him in Honduras, without needing to raise personal support.

Jeff and Nancy, with their children Erin and Evan, came to Honduras in 1999 at a needed time within the Mission's history. With the funds from the Mission's Hurricane Mitch Fund available for use and needing careful, wise disbursement, the Lord has used the Brady's business sense, administrative skills and genuine love for others to put into play a mountain of people wanting to be involved, but needing guidance.

An example of this was seen at the Barrio Botillo housing project on the day of my visit, where 150 new homes are being built. Jeff and his leadership team have organized the finances, charging others with keeping the books. They have organized the new home owners to build their own respective homes, with the help of manager/supervisors from CB churches. They organized material purchases, using CB men to check and re-check distribution. A mini-brick production plant and a large warehouse were also put into place. Also, a mini-grocery store was built which is maintained by Hondurans as part of an overall attempt to not only provide basic staples for the workers, but to also inject simple principles of micro-business and free enterprise. As Jeff comments, "This is desperately needed during Honduras' on-going socio-economic plight." These concepts have further been re-enforced by arrang-

Jeff and Nancy Brady with a family they were able to help – 2001.

ing the growing of crops year-round in acreage adjacent to the new homes. Crops are planted and harvested and then sold in the mini-grocery store. Additional acreage was allocated as a community area or soccer field with the condition that the community counsel of the newly formed *barrio* wrestle with and decide upon its precise use and design, giving them a sense of ownership and self-determination.

These hurricane relief housing projects have not merely dealt with the spiritual, but have also dealt with social needs, such as teaching participants how to get and keep a job; ecological issues, such as planting trees; and sanitation issues, such as teaching new home owners proper waste management. These communities also saw the production of ecologically-friendly septic tanks. Yet, this is not a social gospel! It is Christ's love lived out in practical ways.

The biblical gift of administration, for which Jeff has shown himself a possessor and user, is not merely the facility to shuffle papers on a desk – as we often tend to think due to our western, post-industrial experience. This gift is the ability to comfortably and swiftly mobilize and administer people. Jeff does this with such an ease that the power certainly comes from the Spirit. Naturally, this is what the Lord had in mind in dispensing this gift – both during the 1st century as well as during the 21st century – to mobilize the saints. For this, the Kingdom of God has been blessed with the Bradys on the Honduran north coast. Workers have been mobilized and in such a way that the local indigenous leadership structures have not been skewed nor abused. The Bradys have mobilized others to fit and function like a well-working, well-lubricated machine. They have gotten others involved and not merely done the work themselves.

This reflects Jeff's mild mannered way of being able to get along with others and yet being able to spur them on to obedience to Christ without necessarily being the "boss." As part of this, Jeff and Nancy have a keen ability to bond with Hondurans, which stems from a sense of "we love you." While most of us would maintain our closest ties on the field with other North Americans, the Brady's closest relationships are with nationals. And the greatest testimony to this is not simply the way the Bradys live, work and connect with nationals, but the way Hondurans feel at ease and at one with the Bradys. For not having been through the normal track of missions preparation (college, seminary, etc.), the Bradys have evidenced an uncanny knack for living out Christ's own missiological applications that the rest of us (this writer included!) spend years to study and, oftentimes with some effort, apply.

Overall, the Bradys started in missions late in life by ordinary standards. But yet, like Jesus' parable of the laborers who arrived late in the day to the vineyard (Matthew 20:1f), the Master proves to be well pleased. While many Christian businessmen see missions as a once-a-year diversion allocated to their vacation times, the Bradys have used their business success as an entry to full-time on-the-field missions. Good job, Jeff and Nancy.

Other CB Missionaries in Honduras During the Late '90s

- Venancio and Suyapa Mejia served with HRVC radio station. Venancio was the General Manager during the '90s and into the new century.
- Chrysti Reeck served as a nurse stationed at the Hospital Loma de Luz in Balfate, Colón, from around the turn of the 21st century. Chrysti had long been on the field as an MK with Wycliffe Bible Translators, both in Mexico, where as a child she even crossed paths with Debbie O'Connor, and in La Ceiba, where her parents served as translators.
- Marvin and Cristina Rodriguez served as national missionaries doing church planting by extension in and around

La Esperanza, Intubucá from 1999 on into the new millennium. The Mission appointed Rodriguez jointly with the Tegucigalpa association of churches, such that he was essentially sent out by the Honduras churches in joint partnership with the Mission. The Mission took steps to groom Marvin to use the principles of church planting by extension. Within the first year, Marvin saw three churches birthed through the applied concepts of church planting by extension. His three new works that year were Los Pinares, Las Tijeras and Río Grande, all just outside La Esperanza.

➢ Dave Drozak, with his wife Becky and children, served as a medical doctor with Hospital Loma de Luz in Balfate, Colón, from 1999 on into the new millennium. Folks walk from great distances to the hospital for quality care and to hear about the love of Jesus from the staff.

➢ Steve and Michelle Jacott came on with the Mission near the close of the 1990s to serve as teachers at Academia Los Pinares in Tegucigalpa.

➢ Michelle Crotts served for three months as an MTA missionary intern in Copán Ruins during the summer of 2000. It was a time of learning Spanish, connecting with the youth and getting to know not only the Honduran culture, but also the Mission and the CB missionaries. She later returned to Honduras with another mission, focusing on youth work among CB churches in Tegucigalpa. She was an answer to Debbie O'Connor's prayer of four years for a full-time MTA youth specialist.

Missionary intern Michelle Crotts in San Jeronimo de Copán – 2000.

➢ Cory and Erica Keith, with their two-year-old son Seth, arrived in January, 2000, to serve for a two-year term in Copán and Lempira as CB missionaries. They ministered alongside the O'Connors and the Almendarezes in the western mountains. Erica had previously spent six weeks as a single with CB missionaries in La Ceiba back in 1995. Cory also did short-term missions in Brazil before meeting and marrying his best gal.

- Melani Charney served as a missionary trainee alongside the O'Connors for five months in Copán Ruins in 2000-2001, having previously been an MTA Campus Ambassador.

Food for Thought – We see that the Keiths, Andrew Wachsmuth, Debbie O'Connor and Lillian Migliorini (in the Guatemala section) had short-term missionary experience before returning to the field for long-term service. What can we do as a Mission to facilitate on-the-field short-term missionary work?

---

[25] Data for the years 1952 to the late 1970s is based heavily on information provided by David R. Jones, James Clark and others.

[26] Enyart, Paul C., ***Friends in Central America***. Pasadena: William Carey Library, 1970.

[27] Spain, Mildred W., ***And In Samaria.*** Dallas: The Central American Mission, 1954, p. 56.

[28] Hefley, James and Marti, ***Uncle Cam***. Huntington Beach, CA: Wycliffe Bible Translators, 1984, pp. 29f. Also, Steven Hugh, ed., ***A Thousand Trails***. Langley, BC, Canada: CREDO Publishing Corporation, 1984, pp. 45f.

[29] The Black Legend theory among historians relates to attributing the Spanish Catholic rule over Latin America (1500s to 1821) with primarily relations of cruelty and vice on behalf of the Spanish crown.

[30] Nuñez C., Emilio A. and William D. Taylor, ***Crisis in Latin America***. Chicago, IL: Moody Press, 1989.

[31] The Mexican Bible Institute was later re-named the Nogales Baptist Seminary.

[32] This is not a criticism, merely an observable trend among many North American mission agencies throughout the last 100 years.

[33] Missiologist Donald K. Smith during chapel on February 3, 2000 at Western Seminary, Portland, OR.

[34] Recommended reading for all missionaries: ***Missionary Methods: St. Paul's or Ours***, ***The Ministry of the Spirit,*** and ***The Spontaneous Expansion of the Church***, all by Roland Allen. Better still than these and more concise and easier to read is Melvin Hodges, ***The Indigenous Church***, which is still in print at the time of this writing.

[35] The Catholic church essentially had a monopoly on the religious lives of Latin Americans since the 1500s and they did not want to easily give this up. Interesting reading that documents this is ***Marcos Carías' La Iglesia Católica en Honduras (1492-1975)***. Tegucigalpa: Editorial Guaymuras, 1991.

[36] See Panamá section for more details on Howard Erickson.

[37] ***The Challenge***, Wheaton, IL: Conservative Baptist Home Mission Society, April, 1964, p. 4.

[38] The Executive Committee of the new CB association had power to investigate matters in the local churches, which later caused major conflict between many CB churches and the new CB Association.

[39] Missiologist Donald K. Smith during chapel on February 3, 2000 at Western Conservative Baptist Seminary, Portland, OR.

[40] Patterson followed the simple principle that a departure from the primary scene of leadership will oftentimes enhance local leadership mechanisms. Patterson stayed in touch with the leaders by extension – once a month or so.

[41] This section written by George and Denny's eldest daughter, Anne Patterson Thiessen, who lives as a missionary in Mexico with her husband Rob.

[42] The rural churches of the north coast and central mountain region of Olancho used extension principles, while the city churches did not.

[43] Patterson presents the seven principal commands of Christ as: to repent, to be baptized, to love God and others, to give, to pray, to take the Lord's Supper and to teach others.

[44] TEEE, Theological Education and Evangelism by Extension. Patterson adapted TEE to include the extra "E."

[45] Omar and Ada Reyes went on to serve with the CBs in Tegucigalpa. Omar served as an effective pastor in the Miraflores church and also served as radio pastor with HRVC.

[46] Here pastoral subsidies are distinguished from support to board-appointed national missionaries.

[47] Smith, Donald K., "*Dependency.*" An unpublished paper, 1997.

[48] Allen, Wayne, "*When the Mission Pays the Pastor.*" ***Evangelical Missions Quarterly***, Volume 34, Number 2, April, 1998, p. 181.

[49] Neill, Stephen, ***A History of Christian Missions***. London: Penguin Books, 1986, p. 148: "No serious attempt was made to build up an indigenous ministry."

[50] Latourette, Kenneth Scott, ***A History of Christianity***. Peabody, MA: Prince Press, pp. 1285.

[51] Allen, Wayne, "*When the Mission Pays the Pastor.*" ***Evangelical Missions Quarterly***, Volume 34, Number 2, April, 1998, p. 181-2.

[52] During the 1988 Olanchito CB associational meetings, attempts were made by leaders from Tegucigalpa to shut down HEBI.

[53] Due to growth in many directions, the north coast area had come to include the departments of Atlantida, Colón, Olancho and Yoro.

[54] This statement is meant as a generalization regarding all North American missionaries. It is not meant to slight our own CB missionaries in particular.

[55] It is noted that new areas have been opened during the 1980s and 1990s (southern Mexico, Guatemala, Nicaragua, western Honduras, and San José, Costa Rica, among others), but that many new areas are yet to be opened.

[56] Patterson returned to the States to serve the Mission as a trainer of others who were preparing themselves for cross-cultural ministry.

[57] CBHMS's name was changed to Mission to the Americas (MTA) in 1994.

[58] Data from 1999.

[59] Data from 2000.

[60] These two approaches pretty much apply to all the large cities within Latin America.

[61] As we saw in the Guatemala section, the pastoral approach to church planting is seen when the church planter pastors the church during its birthing process, but then turns the work over to someone else later.

[62] Information for this section provided by Ruth Palnick.

[63] Prepared by Victor Almendarez.

[64] To be precise, northern European countries surpassed the USA in sending missionaries until the 1940s, with the USA taking the lead after the Second World War.

[65] Neill, Stephen, ***A History of Christian Missions***. London: Penguin Books, 1986, pp. 151 and 173.

[66] These manuals were originally titled ***Compendium de Preparación Pastoral***, volumes 1-6.

[67] Details for this section were provided by MTA missionary Steve Reed.

[68] See Guatemala section for more details regarding the Ratskys.

Nicaragua –

The Heart of Central America

Humberto and Carmen Del Arca – 1995.

The work in Nicaragua began with a vision. Ever the vision caster, CB missionary Patrick O'Connor prodded fellow missionary Humberto Del Arca unceasingly that new fields must be opened beyond the current regions. Del Arca took two trips with O'Connor to Nicaragua in the early '90s to scout out the area. In time, the vision-seed for a new ministry would birth and grow within the hearts of Del Arca and others. By the grace of God, the seed took root with the result that Del Arca continued to till the soil of God's harvest in Nicaragua. By the end of the 1990s, CB churches had been established with several church buildings built. In 2001 the Mission appointed Rigoberto and Claudia Reyes, to serve as MTA national missionaries near Chinandega, Nicaragua. With Del Arca as his mentor, Rigoberto's vision would be to reproduce the Honduras HEBI model of TEE and CPE.[69] Within the first year, he saw the formation of eight church

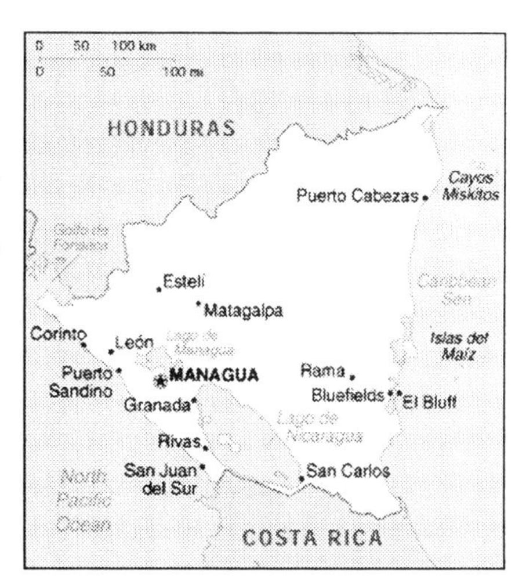

plants. We see from this that great ministries begin with a dream, a burden and a vision.

Food for Thought – What role does vision have in our lives? Are we missionaries who are merely "managers," living out the status quo, or are we visionaries? Do we live out the visions of others or do we ask the Lord for new visions and new opportunities such as the work of Del Arca in Nicaragua?

[69] Church planting by extension.

Costa Rica –

Central America's "Rich Coast"

The Eastern Seaboard of Costa Rica – Limón[70]

The Baptist work in Costa Rica predates the connection with the Mission by many years. The first evangelical work in Costa Rica was started in Puerto Limón over 100 years ago. The church there was known as the Jamaican and Central American Baptist church and was started in the 1880s. It was pastored for many years not only by missionaries from Jamaica, but also by North American missionaries under the direction of the Jamaican Missionary Society. This work was also led for many years by a Rev. Ford, who was a graduate of Spurgeon's Bible School in London, England. He proved to be a man of boundless energy and resourcefulness, and under his leadership the church at one time fostered 15 mission churches. All of these daughter churches were located in the province of Limón. These churches were known as the "line churches," as they were located in areas along the railroad line between Puerto Limón and San José.

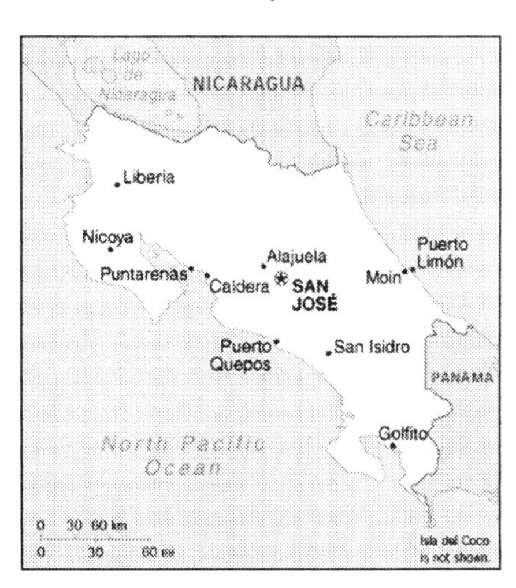

Nearly all of the church members were of black heritage and had moved to Limón from a number of Caribbean and Central American countries. Until 1948, blacks were prohibited by law from living outside the

Costa Rica "Line" Churches – so named because they were along the rail line (upper left). Clockwise from upper right: Matina, Old Harbor, Zent, Waldeck – 1960's.

province of Limón and thus, many blacks lived within the province.

Toward the end of Pastor Ford's ministry, many of the churches were absorbed by the Southern Baptists. Others – including the principle church in Puerto Limón – elected to affiliate with the CBs.

Pastor Ford's ministry had not done much to develop a strong, trained laity. As a result, many churches cried for leadership. It was at this juncture in 1965 that their first request was sent to Wheaton. Dr. Jones from the Mission head office asked Lloyd Lindo to consider relocating to Costa Rica. Lindo and his wife, Millicent, had been serving with the Mission in the Chicago inner city. Lindo would spend six months in Limón and would be instrumental in paving the way for other missionary couples.

Alvin and Celestine Quamina also arrived soon thereafter. Since Alvin was from the island of Trinidad in the West Indies and from a long line of Baptist ministers dating back to 1912, it was thought that he would fit right in with the culture of the folks of Limón. Unfortunately, his sub-cultural background and social orientation proved to be in conflict with the majority of the church members.

Joe and Betty Hutton were the next CB couple to minister in Limón and would cement the growing relationship between the Limón churches and the Mission. In arriving on the eastern seaboard of Costa Rica, the Huttons assumed the ministry responsibilities of Pastor Alvin Quamina, who in conjunction with the arrival of the Huttons was appointed as a national missionary[71] to his motherland of Trinidad Tobago.[72] The Huttons went on to serve in Limón from around 1967 to 1969. Joe and Betty had previously been in Puerto Rico for nearly seven years and returned there in 1969.

John and Hope Miller were appointed to Limón in December of 1969 and arrived in November 1971. After eight months of language study in San José, they started their full-time ministry. The thrust of their ministry was evangelism, church development and leadership training. During their four years in Limón, they saw significant growth from both the main church in Puerto Limón as well as from the line churches. Due to personal needs relating to their children, the Millers returned to the States in 1975.

Joan and Hope Miller.

Following the Millers, Joseph and Josephine Stephens were appointed to the work and served one term in Limón. The Stephens were instrumental in beginning COSTACAD, which focused on raising up lay persons for leadership.

Jack and Sally Hawthorne followed the Stephens in the ministry, serving in the area for a few years. Like previous missionaries before him, Jack served as pastor at the Limón church. It was during this time that three unique young men were raised up from within the church. All three were sent to the States for further study. One of these young men, Patrick Tinkam, later became a CB missionary and returned to pastor the Limón church.

Ministry Near the Capital

Appointed with the Mission during the 1990 annual meetings, Patrick and Connie Tinkam eagerly raised their needed support and got off to his home and native land. While Patrick loved the Limón area and while they enjoyed several fruitful years of ministry there, they both felt that it was necessary to extend the CB ministry to the central valley of the capital city – San José. The Tinkams felt that the relationship between the Mission and the line churches was merely centered on providing church leadership and funds for the line churches and that a greater vision had to be pursued beyond their current borders. With this as their burden and vision, they moved to Cartago (just outside San José) and began ministry in a spiritually barren area, called Tres Ríos. They began outreach and discipleship, and also implemented plans for the normal procedures for a new church plant. While they had much to hope for, Connie was diagnosed with cancer and ordered to return to the States *pronto* for surgery. In light of this and other complications with Connie's health, the Tinkams relocated in Arizona where they became engaged in church planting and leadership training in the Tucson area.

Prior to the Tinkam's departure, CB missionaries Ken and Dee Holcomb were in preparation to move to Costa Rica. Ken was already a well-seasoned veteran missionary, having completed nearly 25 years with the Mission in northern Mexico and central Arizona. The Holcombs had anticipated a ministry with the Tinkams, but with the Tinkam's sudden departure, the Holcombs would be *solo* in Costa Rica for the time being. After a series of exposure trips to Central America, the Holcombs began their move to Costa Rica with a ten-day drive through Mexico and Guatemala. They then made their way to Costa Rica, arriving in November 1998. The Lord permitted them to purchase a home and they soon began a church-planting ministry outside the capital city in Lagos de Lindora. Lagos de Lindora is an area of nearly 400 homes with no church of any kind. The Lord blessed the work and within a short time the new CB church, with the assistance of monies raised through the Mission, purchased a place of its own for worship.

With their years of service in ministry under their belt, the Holcombs knew how to put into practice the essential steps toward the start of their ministry: they made disciples. While many missionaries often have a well laid out diagrammatic outline regarding the church planting task, the Holcombs stuck to the basics of pouring their lives into others, asking the Lord to stir in the hearts of others and thus form a living, functioning church. Making disciples proves to be the organizational aspect to the future church as it puts into place relationships for the new body that will go far toward establishing a deeply rooted, well grounded ministry. The Spirit, in His mysterious way, seeing this obedience in the church planter and wanting to use these firm spiritual roots, will often create, confirm and reinforce the inner spiritual oneness of the new church, which is the "organismal" aspect. Mere man cannot birth an organism, only the Spirit can. While we disciple mature men and carry out church planting plans with the hope and prayer for an end which looks something like a God-honoring, Bible-based church, we none-the-less ask for, count on and testify to the Spirits role. It is this role of the Spirit which the Holcombs looked to and relied upon. God honored their faith in action and raised up a new church.

Like most CB missionaries, the Holcombs have had a vision beyond their immediate region. In this light, the Holcombs have helped with a church plant among the Cavecar Indians in Southern Costa Rica. At the time of this writing, they also hope to take exposure trips to Panamá to check out the Kingdom needs there.

---

[70] Information for this section provided by MTA missionaries John Miller and Patrick Tinkam.

[71] ***The Challenge***, Wheaton, IL: Conservative Baptist Home Mission Society, September, 1969, p. 1.

[72] While the appointment took place, a firm CB ministry in Trinidad never came to pass.

Panamá –

Gateway to South America[73]

The Ministry in Panamá – from 1953 to 1967

Howard and Cally Erickson were the first CBHMS missionaries to Panamá, arriving on the field in 1953. At the time, "the isthmus," as it is known, numbered 800,000 souls.[74] For a number of years, Howard worked primarily with radio station HOXO as a technician and program specialist. This was their principle focus in Panamá. Their previous mission experience was with CBFMS in the Philippines, where Howard served as a radio engineer from 1948-52. Cally was always at his side, assisting him with preparing programs and doing bookkeeping for the station.[75]

HOXO was in Llano Bonito. This station built its own transmitter and anticipated a growing ministry. The station was a joint ministry venture by the Latin American Mission and the World Radio Missionary fellowship, which ran HCJB of Quito, Ecuador, at the time.[76]

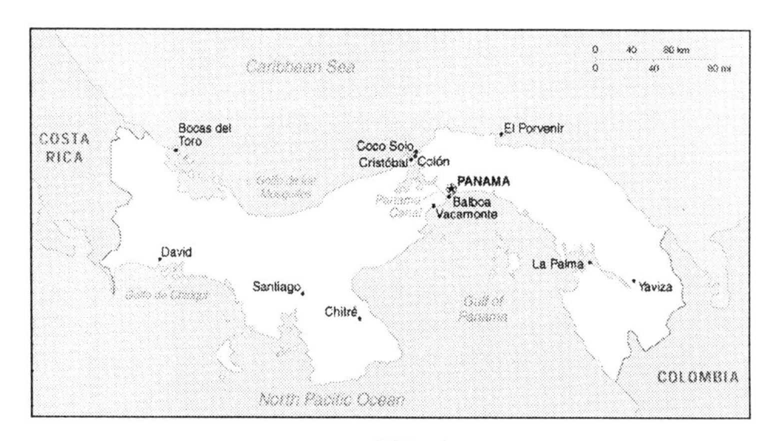

There was so much need and so much to be done. So, in the garage of the radio station, the Ericksons began a children's work, which led to a new church group. This ministry complemented other outreaches, such as a military outreach in Fort Clayton. The new church was bilingual and targeted West Indians. The West Indians were English-speaking black Panamanians who had migrated from the Caribbean Islands decades before in search of non-slave-like conditions. It is remembered that Erickson was not so much a church planter but an engineer. So, starting the ministry with the kids was an "extra." With the many needs around them, the Ericksons desired to do something as an outreach. The Lord blessed them and a small building was later erected and regular meetings were held.

Food for Thought – Reaching out to children is vital and oftentimes an entry point in the lives of others. It has proven to be a good strategy for many church planters. How should a church planter integrate a desire to reach out to children with a need to focus on faithful men so as to prepare them for leadership?

In the late 1950s after the Ericksons had been in Panamá some time, Charles and Joan Moore and their family moved to Panamá. They were appointed in 1956 and, following deputation, spent a year in Costa Rica acquiring the language. The Moores arrived in Panamá with great enthusiasm to assist the Ericksons. Having previously served with the Conservative Baptist Foreign Mission Society in South America, they were assigned to a church-planting ministry. They would work in the Llano Bonito area with the Ericksons, taking over the Sunday school, which had been started by the Ericksons.

The leadership of this young church was provided briefly by the Moores, but was soon followed up with further missionary leadership. While 11 baptisms were recorded in the first few years, the church was weak and was never officially organized. National men were hard to find to lead the church. As missionaries took it upon themselves to provide pastoral leadership, further growth toward localized leadership was hampered. This is neither to cast judgement nor to criticize. To the contrary, our missionaries are commended for experiencing what all missionaries face: the challenge to locate and raise up national men. Oftentimes, a cross-cultural ministry will rise or fall on this point. As North Americans lead churches on the field, the church tends to take on a North American flavor. Nationals, preferring a more local flavor, will often resist such flavoring and will leave in search of a more indigenous church and respective leadership opportunities.

The Halls arrived in Panamá in February 1963, having been appointed with CBHMS in 1961. Before arriving on the isthmus, Bob and Doris spent the better part of 1962 in Honduras taking David Jones's place on the north coast of Honduras while David and his family were on furlough. Bob and Doris had also served with CBFMS in Argentina before coming on with CBHMS.

Arriving in what many consider the hottest and most humid of the "Banana Republics," the Halls were eager to win Panamanians for the Lord and so quickly got into the work. Due to the precedent, the Halls took over the guidance of the Llano Bonito church. Yet, sadly, when they took it over, there were only two of the baptized believers left, as many of the members had left.

The Halls continued to hold bilingual meetings. Meetings were in English for the adults and Spanish for the children. A shift was made to have all programs in Spanish. A shift was also made in that more evangelism was emphasized in both the Llano Bonito area as well as in the neighborhood where the Halls were residing.

The grace of God shined down from Heaven as Mr. Hall realized the need to look for a local man to lead the church. The church desperately needed to look more Panamanian. The Halls sought and found a fine national pastor. He and his wife moved to Llano Bonito and took over the major responsibilities of the church. This adjusted leadership structure would serve the local church well in light of what the Lord knew was coming down the path.

In January 1964, riots broke out between Panamá and the Canal Zone. The subsequent breaking of diplomatic relations between the U.S. and Panamá was a severe time for the foreign missionaries. Unrest was at a peak and served to further persuade the Halls to completely nationalize the Llano Bonito church. Such nationalization was long overdue. It was around this time that the Moores returned to the States.

With tensions from the riots simmering down as the months drew on, the Halls recognized a new need for outreach.[77] Studying the situation and reflecting upon the overall needs, they recognized an entirely neglected field. They recognized that nowhere in Panamá was an effort being directed to the professional class. This burden weighed heavily on their hearts. After a long time of prayer, they put a strategy into action. Their approach was to begin weekly meetings in a location that would not intimidate professionals. They sought a location where their audience would be relaxed and yet open to spiritual matters. Because of the great prejudice against churches and "church type" buildings, they selected an office space on the ground floor of the Hotel Continental in downtown Panamá City, an area of the largest concentration of the professional and middle class. This location seemed ideal as it was in the Panamanian "Neutral Zone."

This approach saw fruit. In 1965, the Centro Bíblico de Panamá was founded. During their first year, many avenues were sought to meet the people. One of the most effective was the offering of English lessons. They taught English using the

Bible as a text. Within the first year or so, nearly 250 people from all walks of life enrolled, from janitors to judges and maids to merchants. Catholics, Buddhists, Muslims and Jews participated. It was a time of great hope. Not only this, but the Bible Center also had become a gathering place for young people from the University and from various high schools close by. The Bible Center became recognized by the people of the area. This was a dream come true. The Halls were thrilled to be a part of many lives being saved and changed.

As part of an overall approach to form a new congregation, the Halls held weekly Sunday church services. They also had daily activities. Women's Bible classes were held, counseling sessions were provided and English classes were available too. Another approach was to sell Christian literature.

In 1972, Bob and Doris resigned from CBHMS, though they continued to live and minister in Panamá for many years. 1972 seemed to mark the end of the CB missionaries in Panamá. The Ericksons had left for Honduras to serve a vital role in setting up HRVC before retiring in 1974. The remaining CB missionaries in Panamá also resigned.

During the January, 2001 MTA board meetings held in La Ceiba, the Mission appointed Luis Matute, a Honduran national from La Ceiba, Honduras, to re-open Panamá.

---

[73] This chapter is based largely on Mr. Hall's CBHMS Panamá Field Report, 1967.

[74] Population statistics for the year 2000 place Panamá as having nearly 3 million people.

[75] ***The Challenge***, Wheaton, IL: Conservative Baptist Home Mission Society, April, 1954, p. 4.

[76] Ibid.

[77] ***The Challenge***, Wheaton, IL: Conservative Baptist Home Mission Society, October, 1967, p. 3.

Puerto Rico –

The "Rich Port" of the Caribbean[78]

A Bit of Background

During his first bold and dangerous trek across the Atlantic from Spain to discover a new route to the Far East, Columbus landed in Puerto Rico in 1493. Spain controlled the island for more than 400 years and it had long ago been determined to be a "rich port" for centralized control of the area and for the shipment of slaves to the New World. In 1898, it was turned over to the U.S. at the close of the Spanish-American War. The people of the island have since been declared U.S. citizens and Puerto Rico has become a commonwealth of the U.S. with the attributes of both a state and a territory. As U.S. citizens, Puerto Ricans enjoy the freedom of travel to and within the U.S.

Due to the Spanish influence, Roman Catholicism has long been a part of the cultural and religious tradition of the people. It was in this context that the Lord moved among the CBs to begin a work on the island. Joe and Betty Hutton opened up the

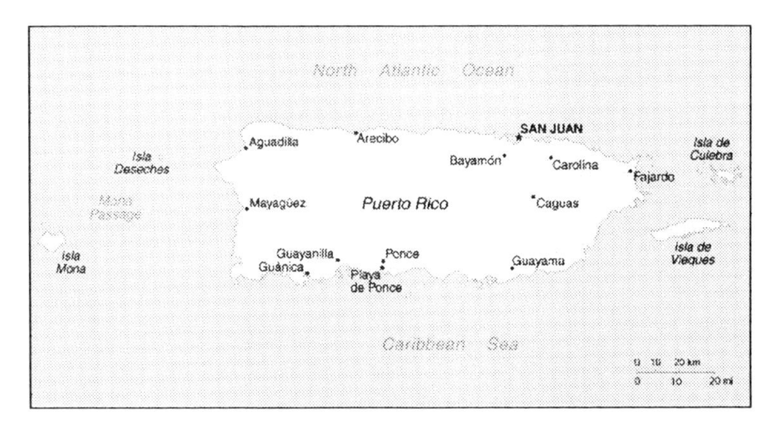

CB ministry in 1958. They arrived in the western port city of Mayagüez. As we shall see, others followed their lead in the 1960s: Roy and Del Anderson arrived in 1962 and John and Barbara Nichols arrived in 1964.

The Huttons and the Andersons

Joe and Betty Hutton's first two years were spent learning Spanish and in helping out in La Iglesia Independiente, a small break-off from the main Presbyterian church in Mayagüez. In 1960, Joe took over the leadership of the small group that became the nucleus of the first CB church in Puerto Rico. This was on the outskirts of Mayagüez in the area known both as La Quinta and Mayagüez Arriba. Joe was the principle leader, but soon passed the baton to Roy Anderson.

Roy and Del Anderson arrived in Mayagüez in 1962. Under Roy's leadership the church grew and was soon organized. The La Quinta group was organized in 1963 as La Iglesia Bautista de Mayagüez Arriba. A simple wooden building was erected.

Church planters often say that the best time for a church to start a daughter church is within the first year of life of the mother church. This proved to be the case for La Iglesia Bautista de Mayagüez Arriba. While still young and energetic, this church began to reach out to different homes in an area not far from Mayagüez called Liceo. This small group in Liceo was organized in December of 1963 as Puerto Rico's second CB church, La Iglesia Bautista El Buen Pastor. Property with a small log cabin was purchased for this church in 1964.

This log cabin was used by the Liceo church as it's first location – 1964.

New to the field in 1964, Jack and Barbara Nichols assisted with the Liceo church with Jack taking over the pastoral leadership. Maintaining the momentum, an additional church was started in the Mayagüez area with the result that the Conservative Baptist Association of Puerto Rico was incorporated with three member churches.

In 1965, the five year old La Quinta church saw the pastoral leadership baton passed to a Puerto Rican who actually came from Philadelphia, Carlos Cortés.

> **Food for Thought –** At what point in the life cycle of a cross-cultural church plant should the baton of leadership be passed to local men? Should such a "baton" be passed on to the nationals or should it be in their hands from the start?[79]

There are many ways to get a church off the ground. While being cautious to recognize the energies of the missionaries in Puerto Rico during these early years, many suggest that new churches should not begin public services until a local man is in place as the leader. Such an approach fosters localized leadership from the start and is more likely to engender not only a culturally correct flavor for the church, but also foster inner mechanisms that do not rely on expatriates. In light of this, many suggest that missionaries should not function within primary posts of pastoral leadership, but should prepare locals for such posts from the start. That is not always possible, but it is what is aimed for. In all likelihood, the missionaries in Puerto Rico at the time looked for such local men and struggled to find them. When unable to find local men, missionaries must often choose the option of pastoring the church so as to provide for the new church's needs. It is a hard choice, yet godly leaders must often make this choice to provide for the Kingdom of God in their sector.

It was in 1965 that the Conservative Baptist Seminary was inaugurated by Roy and Jack. They began with three full-time students, with Roy and Jack serving as instructors. One of these young students, José Irizarry, became a pastor-in-training for the Liceo church.

In 1966, Joe Hutton began a work in Cabo Rojo, near Mayagüez. The small group was organized as a church in 1966, but later disbanded due to a lack of growth. In June of 1967, the pastor of the La Quinta church, Carlos Cortés, left the CBs and persuaded the church to join the Southern Baptist Association, who until then had not been working in the western area of Puerto Rico. It was around this time that the Huttons left Puerto Rico to help out on the eastern seaboard of Costa Rica for two years.

In 1968, Lyle and Marilyn Hoag arrived in Puerto Rico and took up residence in San Germán, a quaint, rustic, small town 20 miles or so to the east. Lyle assisted with teaching duties at the seminary.

One of the seminary students, David Vélez, became pastor of the church in Liceo, with Nichols serving as his coach and mentor. During 1969, the seminary also held extension classes in the metropolitan area of Bayamón. This did not prove to be feasible, however, and was later dropped. In May of that year, two students graduated from the seminary, José Irizarry and David Vélez. Since that time, a full schedule of classes was discontinued and a partial schedule was inaugurated.

Joe Hutton returned to Puerto Rico in 1969 and took up residence in Carolina, near the capital city of San Juan, with the hope of beginning a church there. However, this failed to materialize as hoped.

In 1970, Oliver Perry and his wife arrived in Puerto Rico and made their home in Lajas, to the south of Mayagüez. The Perrys had been in Honduras with the Mission for nearly 15 years where, as we have seen in the Honduras section, Oliver had worked with leadership training.

It was around this time that Roy Anderson moved to Arecibo with the hope of beginning a church in that northern city. This proved to be unproductive, however, and this scattering of the missionary force over such a wide geographical area was determined by the missionaries at the time to be the reason that set back the thrust of CB ministries in Puerto Rico.

Peter Boyko, who had been appointed with the Mission in 1966, took over the leadership of La Iglesia Bautista de Mayagüez Arriba when Roy Anderson left. In this same year, David Vélez terminated his pastorate of the Liceo church and moved to Arecibo. While working as an agronomist for the government, he also began a Baptist church plant out of his home. José Irizarry stepped in as pastor of the Liceo church, and a lay leader took over as director of a church plant in Limón, which Irizarry had been getting off the ground.

Missionary Attrition

The CB missionary team broke up in the early 1970s. The Hoags left in 1970 because of difficulties with the language and the continuing illness of Marilyn. The Andersons left in 1971 in order to work under the Pocket Testament League in Spain, and the Boykos left Puerto Rico soon after, turning over the leadership of La Iglesia Bautista de Mayagüez Arriba to Jack Nichols. The Huttons then returned to the States in 1973 for health reasons. This was soon followed by the departure of the Perrys.

Food for Thought – What are primary causes of missionary attrition? What can be done on the field or home-side to reduce attrition? What can supporting churches do? What can fellow missionaries do?

New Growth

In spite of the missionary departures, church growth took place, especially with the planting of a new CB church in the northwest city of Aguadilla started by Pastor José Irizarry.[80] A new church was also started in Lajas by Wilfredo Vélez, whom the Perrys led to the Lord a few years earlier. This work in Lajas was later incorporated as La Iglesia Bautista de Lajas with Wilfredo Vélez formally called as the pastor. This work would eventually grow into the strongest church among the CBs in Puerto Rico.

In 1974, the group started by José Irizarry in Aguadilla was organized as La Iglesia Bautista de Camaseyes. Meanwhile, Nelson Bonet took over the leadership of the Liceo church where he had been a member.

José Irizarry left the CB pastorate in the mid 1970s to make a new home in the Chicago area where his imprint upon the CBs would continue. In Chicago, Irizarry was offered a position at Moody Bible Institute teaching Spanish. A small handful of future CB missionaries would pass under his tutelage, including Patrick O'Connor and Debbie Papuc who met in class and later married.

During these years Jack Nichols continued to give seminary classes in the evenings and on Saturdays, while also continuing as pastor at the church in Mayagüez. Ultimately, in 1979, Juan Brignoni, who had been assisting Jack Nichols at First Baptist in

Mayagüez, became the pastor of the church, with the result that nearly 20 years after entering the island, all of the churches were led by localized leaders. It was also during this year that Mario Muniz, another seminary student and a member of the Liceo church, became their pastor.

At this point national pastors were in charge of all the CB churches, and Jack Nichols used his time to help mentor them while continuing to give them classroom instruction.

In 1980, the Lajas church built a sanctuary on the outskirts of Lajas. Later they added an educational unit and purchased additional property for future expansion. In 1982, the church called one of its own members, Francisco Santiago, as co-pastor. Francisco would later move to San Juan in order to work with Child Evangelism Fellowship. The church attempted to start new works in two outlying towns, Boquerón and Sábana Grande, but after a time the attempt was given up due to a lack of response.

As we will see in the Dominican Republic section, Jack Nichols began traveling to the Dominican Republic from Puerto Rico in 1983 in order to give assistance to the new CB work there.

Paul and Linda Rickert arrived in Puerto Rico from language school in the fall of 1984. They assisted the pastor of the Liceo church during their first year and also began a training program in each of the churches.

Puerto Rico team. Left to right: Pastor and Mrs. Wilfredo Vélez, pastor of the Baptist Church of Lajas, Rev. and Mrs. Jack Nichols and Rev. and Mrs. Paul Rickert – 1985.

In 1985, the First Baptist Church of Mayagüez had to tear down their building due to termite damage. It was during this year that the CBHMS board and staff held their semi-annual meeting in Puerto Rico.

During the years of 1986 and 1987, the Nicholses endeavored to help the pastor of the First Baptist Church of Mayagüez in what was an increasingly floundering ministry. The pastor was unable to make necessary improvements and the church finally gave him a vote of no confidence. The congregation began using the church building in Liceo, whose pastor, Mario, gave them some spiritual leadership. Also at around this time the Conservative Baptist Association of Puerto Rico ceased functioning as a vital factor in the life of the churches due to a lack of interest and cooperation on the part of two of the four churches.

In 1988, the church in Aguadilla completed its building with the help of a church from Mesa, Arizona. The Rickerts meanwhile moved to San Germán hoping to plant a church there while the seminary continued the program on weekends.

In 1989, for various reasons, La Iglesia Bautista de Mayagüez Arriba formally united with the church of Liceo. However, the two congregations were not able to fuse themselves well into one family and many of the members of the La Iglesia Bautista de Mayagüez Arriba began to meet separately as a house church, sort of beginning the whole process of a new church all over again.

In 1990, Mario, the pastor of the Liceo church, resigned and later left the island. Eventually, a member of the Liceo church, Gabriel Cintrón, stepped forward to become pastor.

It was around this time that Jack and Barbara Nichols relocated to Nogales, Mexico, to work with the Mission there. The seminary training program came to an end, as no new "Timothys" were coming forth from the four established churches.

During the years 1991-1994, Paul and Linda Rickert served the CB churches in various ways. Paul helped the Lajas church begin an Awana program, which continued for many years as a vital part of this church's outreach. He also helped the Liceo church until Gabriel Cintrón took over as the pastor. The Rickerts gave every bit of energy toward starting a new church in San Germán including having "wet-behind-the-ears" Patrick and Debbie O'Connor spend three months there, yet the hope that the small group of believers in San Germán could be developed into a church remained unfulfilled. While Paul got the work off the ground as the pastor, it was not sustained by localized leadership and later was forced to close her doors. Paul and Linda left Puerto Rico at the end of 1994 to work with URBACAD in New York. With their departure, direct MTA involvement in Puerto Rico came to an end.

As of the turn of the new millennium, there were three CB churches in Puerto Rico:

✓ La Iglesia Bautista de Aguadilla

✓ La Primera Iglesia Bautista in Mayagüez

✓ La Iglesia Bautista de Lajas

Through the years, our CB missionaries exerted great levels of energy as they sought to plant churches. The period of growth among the Puerto Rico CB churches peaked in 1984 with 233 members among four CB churches.

---

[78] Information for this section based on the 1987 Puerto Rico field report. Portions were also provided directly by Jack Nichols.

[79] This is not an attempt to criticize a pastoral approach to church planting. It is an attempt to foster interaction regarding leadership development on the field.

[80] Some missiologists have pointed out that too many non-national missionaries in one area overshadow the blossoming of localized leadership and, as a result, inhibit church growth.

Haiti

The CB activity in Haiti has two parts – ministry during the mid '50s to the mid '60s and ministry during the '90s.

Ministry in the 1950s and 1960s[81]

Wallace and Eleanor Turnbull served under the CB banner from 1954 to 1963. Appointed in May 1954 during the annual meetings in Detroit, they had already been serving in Haiti for six years as independent missionaries prior to coming on with CBHMS. They had been supported as independent missionaries by a group of churches in Michigan. Hence, at the time of their appointment with the CBs they already had a rather large work established. Eleanor's mother, Mrs. Bertha "Granny" Holdeman, also worked with them in Haiti. Granny is a whole story in and of herself!

Wallace and Eleanor Turnbull – 1954.

During the tragic experience of Hurricane Hazel in the fall of 1954 in which whole communities were swallowed up by mud slides as a result of the 130-mile-an-hour winds, Wallace assisted the churches and the

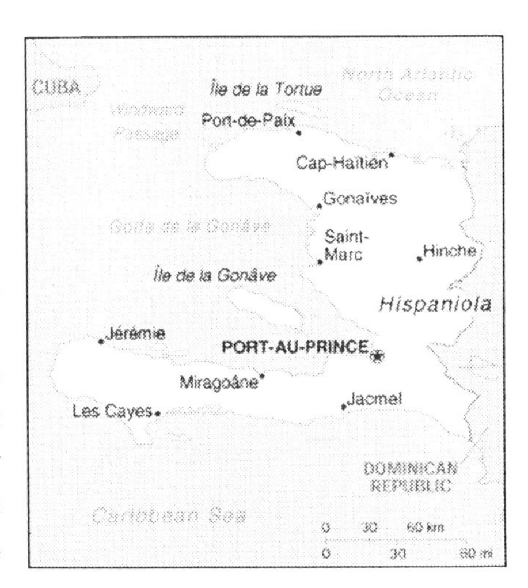

Haitian government greatly with his agile ability to maneuver trips into the mountain areas which were particularly hit hard.[82] Later, the CBHMS ***The Challenge*** newsletter noted in February 1956, that the Turnbulls had taken in more than 60 children who were starving to death as a result of Hurricane Hazel. Many others whom they were unable to rescue died. In 1958, high honor was given to Wallace by the Haitian government through the presidential bestowal of Knighthood in the Order of Honor and Merit. The Chief of Protocol said the Medal of Honor had been awarded because Mr. Turnbull had proven himself faithful to the people in the mountains in a manner that earned the respect and praise of every class of the Haitian people. They went on to add that Wallace had given himself in sacrifice for his adopted country as few would dare to do.

The Challenge noted in July of 1955 that when new converts in Haiti begin living the Christian life, they disposed of their old voodoo charms. Sometimes they would bring their old items of worship to the missionaries. ***The Challenge*** also noted that the Turnbulls were quite effective at winning Voodooists to the Lord. One Voodoo convert named Carnold cornered a Voodoo priest at a Christian wedding reception and insisted that the priest read a portion of the Bible with him. The next day, the priest came to Carnold desiring to be saved. Another man saved from voodooism was Victor. Victor became a very effective preacher and worked in an isolated mountain area telling others of Jesus. This ministry of Victor alone led to the conversion of over 2,000 people in a series of evangelistic campaigns.

In September, 1956, Joe and Betty Hutton were appointed to Haiti, but were later transferred to Puerto Rico in 1958 to help develop that new field for the Mission.

In January, 1957, the entire CBHMS board met in Haiti for their first foreign trip. It was a time of special fellowship at the site of the Turnbulls' home at Fermathe, which was near Port-au-Prince. When "Granny" Holdeman greeted board members of CBHMS in Haiti, she warned them, "We're glad you came to

Haiti, but you'll never be the same when you leave." As with all board meetings abroad, the trip gave board members a chance to see CB mission activities firsthand – ranging from primitive areas where the gospel had seldom been heard to well-established churches pastored by national Christians. One of the highlights was the Sunday service when over 1,000 people from several nearby churches met together for a service that included the marriage of 34 couples and the baptism of 176 converts! Board members were awed, too, as following the service there was a bonfire to burn voodoo fetishes. Board members later testified to a deeper understanding of the real problems of missionary work in Haiti. Granny was right, the CB board members were not the same after their visit to Haiti.

At the same time, Eldon and Joy Ausherman were also serving in Haiti as missionaries. Because they sought to work under the CB banner, they were informally interviewed by the board. At the annual meetings in June 1957, the Aushermans were appointed as well as Fleming and Doris Newcomb and Wilson and Jewell Newcomb. Wilson and Jewell did not make it to the field due to medical-related problems. In June 1960, Jack and Barbara Nichols were also appointed to Haiti. In 1962, Fleming and Doris Newcomb resigned from the Mission for personal reasons.

Three Praises

It was in the fall of 1958 that, using their own resources, the CB church members at Fermathe built their much-needed church building. The building seated 1,000 people, with over 1,500 present at the building's dedication. The hard work and sacrifice created new impetus and emotional church-related bonding for the work. This took place as the nationals – poor as they were – used local monies and manpower.

In the fall of 1959, another such experience took place. The CBHMS ***The Challenge*** recorded that the CB church members in Thomazeau had spent a good amount of time gathering building materials for a needed church building. Having met under a thatch roof supported by a few poles, the believers in Thomazeau had patiently collected materials for four years.

The Turnbulls were full of energy and were used greatly by the Lord. The May-June 1961 issue of ***The Challeng***e reported that "the work in Haiti now includes 50 organized churches, 120 preaching stations, 80 national workers, a Bible school with 94 enrolled and medical work." The Turnbulls focused on local church ministries through evangelism, church planting and training pastors. The Turnbulls also focused on local church ministries in various mountain villages using filmstrips as a key strategy for evangelism.[83]

In the early winter of 1961, with only $42 in their church building fund, the members of the CB Passe Reine church in the Artibonite area began the construction of their church building. As part of the overall project, giant mango trees were cut down in order to provide lime for the masonry work. The church service and instruction classes were being held in the back yard of the Aushermans' home. By 1963, the members had finished their church building.

Food for Thought – How can national churches be encouraged to build their own buildings, as in the case of the CB Haitian churches? What takes place when missionaries unwittingly discourage nationals from using local resources by providing too much foreign assistance in this area?

While there was evidence of much growth and potential, it wasn't long before some problems developed. For several board meetings, some of the Haiti missionaries were brought to the USA to meet with the CBHMS board. At another time, a delegation went down to Haiti to try to resolve several issues. It finally came to a head in June 1963. Due to an opposing philosophy of ministry, to differing expectations regarding the nature of the work in Haiti and to several unresolved conflicts regarding ministry details, the Mission decided that, for the betterment of the Kingdom, the Mission would temporarily withdraw from the field of Haiti. It was at this time that the board accepted the resignation of the Aushermans, transferred the Nichols to Puerto Rico, severed the relationship with the Turnbulls and temporarily closed the Haiti field.

After leaving CBHMS, the Aushermans continued with their ministry in Haiti. Through to the end of the century, the Turnbulls continued to have a significant and well-used ministry for God's Kingdom in Haiti, supported by a number of their former CB supporting churches.

Food for Thought – Where should a mission draw the line in the application of ministry church planting models, as applied in different ways by her missionaries on the field?

The Ministry Re-begins in the 1990s[84]

We could not talk about history of the work in Haiti without talking about Jean Max "Francois" Vilmenay. CB ministry in the 1990s was started by this special saint.

Vilmenay was born in Haiti to a very wealthy family. He studied in a sophisticated private school known as San Louis of Gonzagle. Later as a married man, he saw the birth of his two precious daughters. He was then later introduced to and became part of the Communist Party in Haiti.

During this time, he would have nothing to do with God. He did not believe in the existence of God, but rather participated in many questionable affairs. Years later, however, by God's own design, Vilmenay came to know Christ as Savior. The change was quick and dramatic. The change meant having to leave the Communist Party. All those who knew Vilmenay before were surprised by his repentance and new life.

In 1985, Vilmenay realized that in order to work in the harvest of the Lord, he should acquire specialized ministerial training, whereupon he attended Denver Seminary in Colorado.

Finishing seminary in 1992, he applied with CBHMS as a missionary to his native people. With this new start in Haiti, the Mission had new hopes for a dynamic ministry in this needy place. Back in Haiti in 1992, Vilmenay's vision was clear: to tell others about the love of Christ, to prepare leaders and to start new churches. He wanted to do this from a heart of love, justice and compassion for his fellow Haitians. He wanted to be a new revolutionary – not working for the communists, but for the King of kings. By God's grace, two churches were quickly started in his first year back home. While Haiti would have continued to be blessed by the presence of their own true son, Francois tragically and suddenly died of cancer in February of 1996.

Guillomettre Herode – whom Vilmenay had coached in ministry – took over for his mentor and continued in Vilmenay's place with a vision stronger than ever. The Lord has also put into place Vilmenay's younger brother, Robert, to vitally assist with the work to the end that today Guillomettre and Robert work hand-in-hand carrying on the ministry of love and compassion that Francois Vilmenay had begun. Robert Vilmenay, with wife Jean, serves as an MTA missionary.

---

[81] Dick Falconer provided many of the details for this section.

[82] ***The Challenge***, Wheaton, IL: Conservative Baptist Home Mission Society, December, 1954, pp. 1-2.

[83] ***The Challenge***, Wheaton, IL: Conservative Baptist Home Mission Society, January, 1957, p. 3.

[84] Information for this section was provided by CB Haitian leader Guillomettre Herode.

Dominican Republic

Background Regarding the Dominican Republic[85]

In the heart of the Caribbean lies the Dominican Republic. It is a tropical island with imposing mountains, fertile fields and a shoreline fringed in many areas with soft, white sand. The population of the country is estimated at nearly seven million. Santo Domingo, the capital city, gathers nearly two million of this population.

Throughout the latter part of the 20th century, and thus the entire time in which the CBs have been in Central America and the Caribbean, the economy of the Dominican Republic has been terrible. The country depends on U.S. dollars for almost all imported goods. The cost of the U.S. dollar has become more expensive every year, which has made the cost of living very high in a society that has stayed economically impoverished .

While Roman Catholicism is the principal expression of religion, for the last 20 years the country has been exposed to the light of the gospel in a very new way. In the 1980s, the country began to reap what other missionaries had planted for many years.

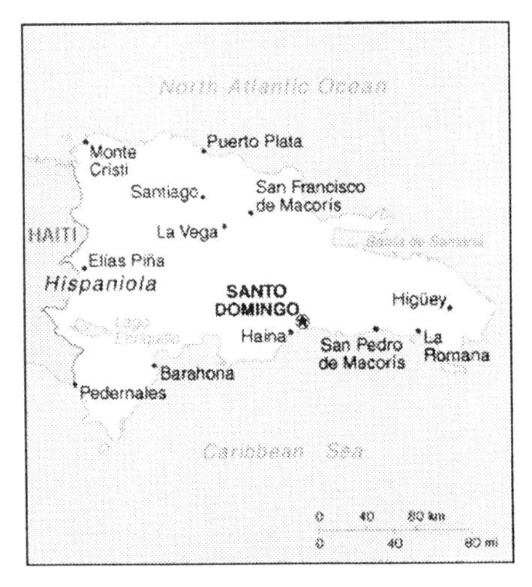

The Entrance of the CBs

The first step in the history of the CBs in the Dominican Republic was taken by Pastor Ismael Ramos of the New York City Broadway Baptist Church. Pastor Ramos had been visiting the island, hoping to see a new work start. In 1981, Pastor Ramos challenged Norman Wetther, then Director of Field Ministries for CBHMS, to visit the Dominican Republic with him. They prayed about the possibility of taking on a new church-planting ministry in Puerto Plata. On behalf of the Mission, Wetther accepted the challenge and thus began the work on the island.

The first national worker was Arcadio Berequete, who officially began to represent the CBs in 1981. It was a short-lived relationship as in 1982 he left the new church plant in the hands of someone else. Berequete turned the ministry over to a young man in the church, Natanael Portes Been. Broadway Baptist Church helped to organize this new church and Been was later appointed as the pastor.

In the early part of 1983, missionary Jack Nichols, who had been serving with the Mission for a number of years in Puerto Rico, began making regular visits to Puerto Plata in order to coach Natanael and in order to set up a program of studies to further Natanael's preparation. At that time, there were around 30 adults and young people who were meeting regularly for worship, instruction and evangelistic outreach. There was also a preschool program being carried on with 35 children. Two of the national pastors from Puerto Rico also aided Jack Nichols in his coaching ministry by traveling by plane to Puerto Plata from time to time for the next few years in order to mentor Natanael. Natanael's preparation was through a combination of programmed texts and intensive courses. It was around this time that the church in Puerto Plata started carrying on an aggressive evangelistic work with children by holding child evangelism meetings outdoors in six different neighborhoods.

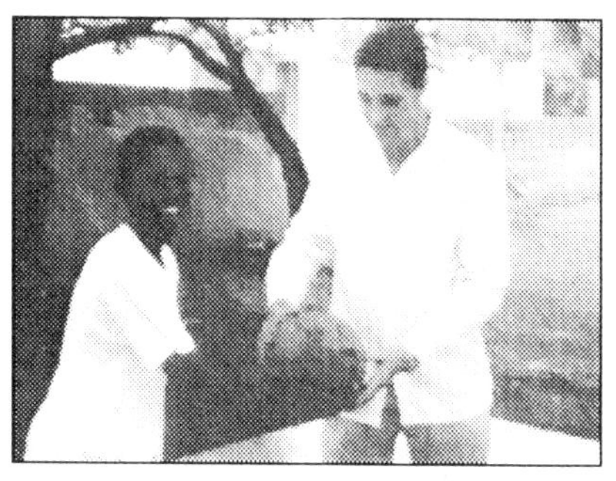

Joaquin Vargas explains the finer points of ball handling during a boys' club activity – 1992.

In December 1985, Joaquin Vargas, who had come to know about the Conservative Baptists while living in New York, was appointed by CBHMS as a Field Minister to begin new churches in the capital city of his native country. Jack Nichols was asked by the Mission to oversee Joaquin during his initial years of ministry in Santo Domingo and to coach him in his preparation.

Joaquin began his work in the northwest section of Santo Domingo where there were about 125,000 people. At the beginning of the ministry, they started having open-air services in parks and in the streets, together with Bible studies in homes. They began holding services in a private school that allowed them to use their facilities for their Sunday services. Through these efforts they began Iglesia Bautista Redención in 1986. Joaquin had previously founded another church in 1979, Iglesia Evangélica Bautista Resurrección, which at this time in 1986 desired entry into the CB movement. This later resulted in the formation of the Association of Conservative Baptist Churches for the Dominican Republic. On January 11, 1988, the CB churches adopted a constitution and a new association was soon incorporated with three founding churches:

- ✓ Iglesia Bautista Conservadora (Puerto Plata), which was pastored by Natanael Portes Been.
- ✓ Iglesia Bautista Resurrección (Santo Domingo), which was pastored by Juan R. Capellan.
- ✓ Iglesia Bautista Redención (Santo Domingo), which was pastored by Joaquin A. Vargas.

In 1987, Paul Rickert began to accompany Jack Nichols to the Dominican Republic. Upon Jack's departure from Puerto Rico in 1990, Paul continued these visits until his own departure from the Caribbean to New York City in 1994.

Academia Biblica Bautista, a CB TEE school, opened its doors in the city of Santo Domingo in January, 1987, to train national leaders for the local churches. They began with 20 students enrolled in the academy.

The church in Puerto Plata was able to purchase a large lot at a very visible site in the town in 1988. Through the help of a church in Minnesota, a beautiful sanctuary was later erected in 1991.

In 1989, the Iglesia Bautista Redención was given a piece of land in the community of Barrio Las Caobas where the church started constructing a multi-purpose building with the help of many groups from the United States. In 1990 Iglesia Bautista Redención was able to move to its new building and has since gained the respect of the people in the area.

Around this time, Félix Abreu, who had been raised up by Joaquin as a disciple, mobilized locals to form a daughter church to Iglesia Bautista Resurrección. Iglesia Bautista de los Mameyes was off to a good start in no time at all, due to the vision and determination of Félix. While this new church was recognized as a CB church, it later elected to affiliate with another mission agency. While the church founded by Abreu left the CB movement, Abreu would find his ministry niche with the CBs. The mid '90s would see Félix Abreu and his wife Amnerys play a significant role on the island for the CBs.

Joaquin Vargas and his family were transferred to Denver, Colorado in 1992 under the MTA banner to pursue a Master of Arts in Missions, which he finished in 1994. Joaquin and his family were then relocated to the Nogales area of northern Mexico and southern Arizona. Joaquin later became an MTA Ministry Specialist for the Colorado area.

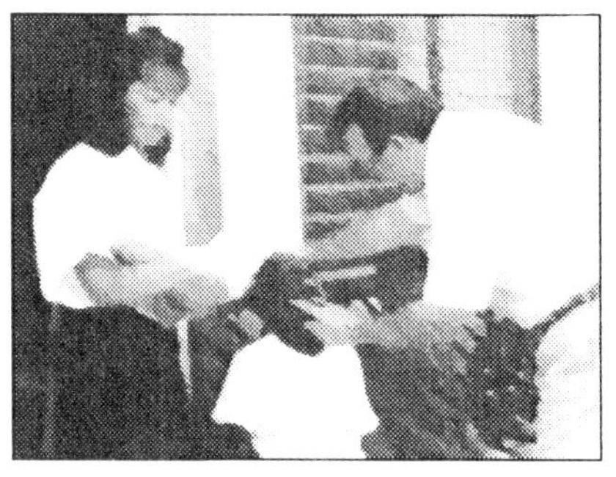

Dr. Steve Brazeau does a quick preliminary dental exam while his wife, Jan, takes notes – 1992.

A new missionary couple arrived in the Dominican Republic in 1991 – Dr. Steve and Janice Brazeau. Steve came with the purpose of working as a missionary dentist. The transition and the adaptation to the new culture was tough, and for a complexity of reasons the Brazeaus decided to return to the United States in 1993.

Early 1994 saw the re-emergence of Félix Abreu. He had been sent by the CBs to Guatemala City in 1990 for a few years of training at CAM International's SETECA seminary. Having returned to the island, Félix was appointed as a Field Minister with MTA with the plan to focus on overall ministry needs. Soon after his return to the island, he quickly established his own discipleship network with such godly men as Victor Arias, Marco Rodríguez and Raisa Montero. These pillars of the faith led the CB work inwardly and outwardly in the areas of music, evangelism, discipleship and preaching. These nationals proved capable in reaching a small but significant portion of their island, living out the mission's vision to evangelize, disciple and congregationalize.

In August of 1994, a sad situation arose in the church of Puerto Plata. The pastor, Natanael, was accused of serious misconduct. When CB Regional Specialist Paul Hutton and Jack Nichols went to Puerto Plata to deal with the situation, Natanael denied any wrongdoing. The church, after refusing to allow Paul and Jack to talk with them, withdrew from the Conservative Baptist Association. Natanael later left the church, with its ministry terribly damaged.

Meanwhile, as part of the overall ministry, Félix with his team of leaders formed what they called their *Centro de Entrenamiento*

Pastoral (CEP). This pastoral training center sought to provide sound leadership training for others who were being stirred by God to work in the Lord's harvest. Their vision was to train others to the end that new churches would be started. Their dream also saw several new churches within the next few years:

- ✓ Iglesia Monte de Los Olivos in the area of Las Canelas came into being in 1995.
- ✓ Iglesia Bautista de Los Alcarrizos in the area of Los Alcarrizos just outside Santo Domingo was begun in 1997.
- ✓ Iglesia Bautista de Bayona in the area of Bayona, also just outside Santo Domingo came into being around 1999.

Their dream also included starting the *Colegio Berea* Institute to train others in the area of drama, music, computer skills and English language skills. All in all, attempts have been made at every angle not only to go forth to make disciples, but also to equip disciples for ministry in a needy world.

As we have seen, it is important that locals "own" and lead their ministry. Local men, as in the case of Félix Abreu and his co-workers, will fare far better in the long run than outsiders[86] in that "they are familiar with local customs, they speak the local dialects, and eat the local food. Moreover, their shops and homes are there. Their farms and families are there. This gives stability to the work, and stability always makes for permanency."[87]

---

[85] Information for this section was provided by Jack Nichols, Joaquin Vargas and Félix Abreu.

[86] As has been the case throughout this book, pointing out that outsiders are oftentimes less effective than trained nationals is not meant to find fault with ourselves as outsiders nor to dismiss the need for foreign missionaries, but to simply observe a trend so that adjustments can be made as we look to the future. The purpose is to learn from the trends we see in our past and make modifications for the future.

[87] Kane, Herbert, ***Twofold Growth***. Philadelphia: China Inland Mission, 1947, pp. 156-7.

Conclusions –

The Value of Historical Review

Western civilization has generally maintained a high view of historical record keeping.[87] As a result, students of western civilization find it relatively easy to survey its past. However, the people of some areas of the world, such as the Indus Valley on the Asian subcontinent, have generally held a low view of history. Have you ever tried to study the myths and legends within Indian history and then attempt to persuade a devout Hindu that legends must be distinguished from historical fact? While historical records permit a speedy distinction between myth and reality, students without this advantage encounter serious obstacles to a scholarly approach of the past. History has value as it permits historical review. Such review enhances growth and progress. The society – and the mission agency – which does not learn from history will repeat it.

This text could have dealt with so much more. More historical synthesis and analysis is afforded, but that, as I have said, will have to be left up to the reader through the "Food for Thought" cues. While I have attempted to provide a geographical and time-line survey, a structure could have followed various ministry approaches: a pastoral approach, as seen through de la Cruz; a bonding approach as seen through Ruegsegger; a helps ministry approach as seen through Reed; a care-giving and extension approach as seen through Dellinger; or a discipling approach as seen through Patterson.

My hope with this history text has been to collect, preserve and to reflect upon our history as a mission. My prayer with this text is that we learn from our past. It is written to affirm our past, yet learn from it. While I have attempted to interact with history objectively as a missiologist, at times it may seem as though my historical review is a bit austere. My intent is not to be harsh, but to interact with our history. Overall, this text celebrates the ways in which our missionaries have lived out the Mission's motto: "...to evangelize, disciple, and congregationalize the unreached...."

Patrick O'Connor

---

[87] From the ancients such as Josephus to our modern day Arnold Toynbee and Lautorette, those of western civilization have exhibited good discipline in taking the time to record history and yet learn from it. Toynbee spent 20 years on his ***A Study of History***.

Index

Other Items of Interest from Enable! Media

Following are some other items published and distributed by ***Enable! Media***. For information, price or to order, contact:

enable-media@servants-inc.org

Preparación para Movilizacion (Preparation for Mobilization) Manuals

These Spanish-language pastoral training manuals are ideal for missionaries who do pastoral training or TEE. Text authored by George Patterson, veteran missionary who spent 21 years in Honduras training pastors in a way that multiplies churches. Manuals were edited, computerized and compiled (with culturally relevant graphics, questions and answers, and practical homework) by Patrick O'Connor, missionary to Honduras under Mission to the Americas. Set of six manuals, Spanish only, 120+ pages each. ISBN 0-9706859-7-1.

Available soon! Preparation for Mobilization manuals on CD-ROM for local print and distribution. Send email for details. ISBN 0-9706859-8-X.

Come, Let Us Disciple the Nations

This interactive e-textbook on CD-ROM is for Christians who desire to plant edifying, reproductive churches or small groups. Content is based on New Testament principles proven on many fields, and illustrated by actual events from many countries. It provides radical training in the form of a fast-paced interactive novel. Authored by George Patterson, church planter and consultant. Programming by Galen Currah, communications consultant and social research specialist. ISBN 0-9706859-0-4.